POLAND
POCKET GUIDE

 **Walking Eye**
mobile app

Discover the world's best destinations with the Insight Guides Walking Eye app, available to download for free in the App Store and Google Play.

The container app provides easy access to fantastic free content on events and activities taking place in your current location or chosen destination, with the possibility of booking, as well as the regularly-updated Insight Guides travel blog: Inspire Me. In addition, you can purchase curated, premium destination guides through the app, which feature local highlights, hotel, bar, restaurant and shopping listings, an A to Z of practical information and more. Or purchase and download Insight Guides eBooks straight to your device.

TOP 10 ATTRACTIONS

KRAKÓW
The former capital of Poland is still the country's artistic and cultural centre and its most popular tourist destination. See page 34.

TATRA MOUNTAINS
With their spectacular peaks they are a hiker's paradise. See page 65.

WIELICZKA SALT MINES
With its extraordinary, ornately carved chambers, this Unesco World Heritage Site is a must see. See page 57.

WARSAW
A wonderful capital city, where history and culture come alive. See page 8.

ZAMOŚĆ
Modelled on Italian trading cities, the Old Town is a 16th-century Renaissance jewel. See page 67.

GDAŃSK
The birthplace of the Solidarity Movement. See page 92.

SOPOT
Poland's lively summer capital. See page 102.

MALBORK CASTLE
Built by the Teutonic Knights and one of Europe's biggest strongholds. See page 103.

KAZIMIERZ DOLNY
A confection of Renaissance and Mannerist houses. See page 71.

KAZIMIERZ
Krakow's former Jewish quarter is re-inventing itself while not forgetting its past. See page 50.

A PERFECT TOUR

Day 1

To the dragon hill
Tour the Royal castle on Wawel hill, have lunch in Kawiarnia Pod Baszta, then visit the cathedral where Poland's kings were crowned. You might catch a short classical concert in one of the Old Town churches before dinner at Krakow's oldest restaurant, Wierzynek (see page 149).

Day 2

Students & synagogues
Enjoy a café in Rynek Główny, before exploring the Old Town. Café Camelot is nice for lunch (see page 147). Later, go to Kazimierz. Dine to the sound of live Jewish music at Klezmer Hois.

Day 4

Warsaw rebuilt
From the top of the Soviet Palace of Culture you get an excellent view of Warsaw, with its modern skyscrapers and rebuilt Old Town. Take a tram to the Warsaw Rising Museum and then walk east through the streets of the former ghetto, for a more light-hearted afternoon in the Old Town, taking lunch in the Rynek Starego Miasta.

Day 3

Medieval mall
Spend the morning searching for souvenirs in the Sukiennice, Krakow's medieval market building, before continuing to Warsaw by internal flight or train.

Day 5

Royal route
Visit the Royal Castle in the morning then take a stroll down from Plac Zamkowy, passing Warsaw University, and stopping for a visit to the National Museum or the Chopin Museum. Take a break for a coffee or lunch on Nowy Świat.

Day 7

Historic Toruń

Walk around the medieval city walls to see Toruń's leaning tower, then visit the museum where its most famous son, Copernicus was born, and marvel at the stars in its Planetarium. In the evening hear live folk music as you eat at Karczma Spichrz (see page 153).

Day 10

Beach life

Frequent trains from Gdańsk will take you to lovely seaside resort of Sopot. Here you can relax on the beach, take a walk along its pier or explore the many nature trails in the area by bike or on foot. Eat at Bulaj (see page 153) on the beach and enjoy the laidback atmosphere.

Day 6

Palace on the Water

Take a trip to downtown Warsaw to admire the beautiful Łazienki Palace and enjoy an afternoon in the peaceful gardens, where locals come to relax. Later, take the train to Toruń.

Day 8

Malbork Castle

An early train from Toruń Głowny will get you to Malbork in less than three hours. Spend the day at the castle, the massive brick stronghold of the Teutonic Knights, before taking an evening train to Gdańsk. Dine at the riverside Restauracja Barytka (see page 152).

Day 9

On the waterfront

Follow the Royal Route from Upland Gate to the Golden Gate before plunging into more recent history at the European Solidarity Centre, not far from the shipyards. Dine in old Gdańsk at Restauracja Targ Rybny (see page 153) in the fish market.

CONTENTS

INTRODUCTION

Despite being more than a thousand years' old, Poland's survival is something of a miracle. Its boundaries have been continually redrawn over the course of eight centuries. Then suddenly it disappeared from the map. Between 1795 and 1918, Poland, wedged in the middle of Europe, ceased to exist. Partitioned for a third time at the end of the 18th century by Prussia, Austria and Russia, Poland became the object of a tug-of-war between more powerful states.

And then the real tragedy occurred. Hitler and the Nazis invaded Poland, launching World War II, then extinguished many of its cities and eradicated 20 percent of its people, including nearly its entire Jewish population of three-and-a-half million – until then the largest Jewish community in Europe. Wars have befallen many countries in modern times, but few have been as thoroughly ravaged as Poland.

Pyramid above the Renaissance Cloth Hall, Kraków

Yet Poland rebuilt itself from the rubble of war. From photographs, paintings, architectural drawings and the memories of its grief-stricken survivors, Poles reconstructed the Old Towns of Warsaw and Gdańsk brick by brick, only to suffer four decades of Soviet-imposed Communist rule. Yet Poland asserted itself once more.

In the 1980s, the trade union movement Solidarity (Solidarność) helped to trigger the demise of Communism in Poland and throughout the Soviet bloc. Poland has survived with its culture, language, spirit and most of its territory intact. In 2004 it joined the European Union, as a modern, independent nation.

HISTORIC CITIES

Largely rural, Poland has great tracts of wilderness and primeval forest in its 23 national parks. However, the country is perhaps best known for ancient towns rich in history and architecture. Kraków, which survived unscathed from the war, is a splendid medieval city (it was the royal capital for 500 years), with a magnificent market square, hill-top castle, and one of Europe's oldest, most prestigious universities.

Warsaw, Poland's largest city by far and its commercial and political capital, is not the bleak grey morass of Communist days. It may still be a little harsh on the eyes in places, but it is undeniably beautiful in others, and perhaps best expresses Poland's current crossroads. A 20-minute walk can take you from the Royal Castle to a monolith of Stalinist architecture to the gleaming headquarters of international companies banking on Poland's emergence as a major European player.

While Warsaw's Old Town is an astonishing phoenix-like fable of reconstruction, Gdańsk's historic centre is even more alluring, its Royal Way a loving restoration that defies the imagination. No matter how many times you stroll through the medieval layouts of these cities over cobblestoned streets, gazing at stunning examples of Gothic, Renaissance and Baroque architecture created, incredibly, as late as 1953, you cannot help but be amazed. The buildings look genuinely old; it is as though the indefatigable Polish people willed their authenticity.

Smaller towns can be just as impressive. Zamość is a perfect Renaissance town with one of the most photogenic main squares in the country. Zakopane is an Alpine-style town carved out of wood at the foot of the High Tatras, the highest peaks of the Carpathian Mountains, within easy range of great hiking and skiing. Toruń, the home of the great astronomer Nicolaus Copernicus, is a feast of red-brick Gothic architecture, while Poznań, a determined trade centre, combines commerce with authenticity in its extraordinary Old Market Square.

POPULATION AND RELIGION

Poland is a nation of 38.5 million. Over 90 percent of the population call themselves Catholic (but less than 40 percent are practising) and they are more conservative than many of their Western European neighbours. Throughout history, Poland has been incredibly cosmopolitan, with Germans, Jews, Lithuanians, Belarusians, Armenians and Ukrainians living there. During the Second Republic (1919–39), only two-thirds of the population were ethnic Poles. It has also traditionally been a land of religious tolerance. When medieval Europe was rocked by religious wars, Poland was a safe haven for Jewish, Protestant and Orthodox refugees – making the intolerance later inflicted by Germany on Polish ground all the more terrible.

Today, Poland is unusually homogenous in terms of ethnicity: some 98 percent of the people are Poles. The Jewish

Green Credentials

Almost one third of Poland is covered by forest, mostly pine, spruce and mixed deciduous and coniferous trees.

A winter scene in the Tatra Mountains

population was reduced to 250,000 after World War II, and today there are only a few thousand Jews living in Poland. The largest minority groups are Lithuanians, Ukrainians and Belarusians.

Literacy rates are high, at a shade under 100 percent. Poles are well-educated, and young people in the larger cities speak good English (much more so than German or Russian). They're up-to-date on fashions, trends, music and technology and they welcome visitors with lavish hospitality.

RURAL POLAND

Of course, some parts of the vast Polish countryside are a very different story. Here you'll still see a stubbornly traditional way of life that seems years slower than city life. Roads are lined with wooden shrines, erected by people intent on manifesting their devotion. Even if you're not planning on travelling through the countryside, you can get a good taste of rural life by visiting a *skansen*, or ethnographic museum, which showcases Polish country life and historic houses in open-air exhibitions.

A BLEND OF EAST AND WEST

Poland's history as a territory coveted by great powers all around it ensured that the north–south divisions often seen elsewhere are, here, primarily east–west divisions. The west is more Germanic, organised, pragmatic and industrious, while the East has a reputation of being more Russian – which means, in short, relaxed, cultural and introspective.

There has always been a cultural struggle between East and West in Poland. The Poles are a Slavic people, like their Ukrainian and Russian neighbours to the east. Yet their historical and cultural connections to the West are formidable. The Catholic Poles first took their religious cues from the West in the 10th century, and cultural epochs basic to Western Europe – the Enlightenment and the Renaissance, for example – were just as much a part of Polish society. The shared identity, as well as the uneasy conflicts, between East and West, have defined this land in ways that go far beyond geography.

CHOPIN

Frédéric Chopin (1810–49) was born in Żelazowa Wola, just outside Warsaw, to a French father and Polish mother. He spent his youth in the capital but also learned all the folk songs and dances of the surrounding villages, which he utilised in almost all his later works. He made his debut as a classical pianist when still a boy, playing in elegant salons. In the autumn of 1830 he left Warsaw, and when the Russians occupied Warsaw the following year, Chopin settled in Paris. In 1836 he met the novelist George Sand, who looked after him during his years of ill health. In 1847, George Sand finally left him. Lonely, ill and poor, he fled to London, where he gave his last public performance. Returning to Paris, he died of tuberculosis.

A NATION OF TRIUMPHS

Poland has enjoyed glorious achievements in the arts and sciences. It claims such greats as the composer Frédéric Chopin, the novelist Joseph Conrad, Marie Skłodowska-Curie (Nobel Prize winner in chemistry and physics) and the Nobel Prize winners in literature Henryk Sienkiewicz, Władysław Reymont, Wisława Szymborska and Czesław

Poland's Baltic coast offers wide sandy beaches

Miłosz. In 1932 the country was the first to crack Germany's Enigma code, a feat many believe to have shortened World War II and to have prevented a nuclear holocaust in Europe.

LIFE POST-COMMUNISM

Poland has made incredible strides in the years since the break-up of Communist Europe in 1989. Its people are intensely proud of Copernicus, who 'stopped the sun and moved the Earth' and revolutionised the way we understand our universe and they revel in the fact that Poland signed the second-oldest Constitution delineating government powers, after the United States. They recognise the role that a little-known shipyard electrician in Gdańsk by the name of Lech Wałęsa had in indelibly changing the events of the second half of the 20th century. As a nation, they turned out in great adoring hordes for the late Pope John Paul II, while the older generation still live with the horrors of death-camp atrocities committed on their soil. Poland may only now be developing as a world travel destination, but it is certainly no stranger to the world stage.

A BRIEF HISTORY

Poland's war-torn, almost incomprehensibly fractured history plays out like an epic novel – occasionally triumphant, frequently sad and tragic. Over a millennium, Poland evolved from a huge, economically powerful kingdom to a partitioned nation that ceased to exist on world maps for over 120 years, and finally to a people and land at the centre of the 20th century's greatest wars and most horrific human tragedies. But Poland has survived, with its culture, language and most of its territory intact, and today Poles, who entered into the European Union (EU) in 2004 and NATO in 1999, are taking their place at the forefront of post-Communist Central Europe.

FOUNDATIONS OF THE POLISH STATE

The region that would become Poland, a great plain sandwiched between the Wisła (Vistula) and Odra (Oder) rivers, has been inhabited since the Stone Age by migratory tribal peoples – among them Celts, Balts, Huns, Slavs and Mongols. Tribal culture reigned, untouched by the more sophisticated civilisation of the Roman Empire. Slavic tribes arrived by the 8th century AD and put down roots; the Ślężanie, Mazowszanie, Pomorzanie and Wiślanie peoples inhabited much of the territory. The Polonian tribe, which settled the area that today is western Poland around Poznań, provided the foundations for the development of a Polish language and nation.

What's in a name?

The Polanie tribe (the Polonians), who lived in the Warta valley not far from Poznań, may have been the people who gave Poland its name. Polanie means 'of the fields'.

Prince Mieszko, leader of the Piast dynasty that ruled the Polonians, undertook the bold step of unifying the Polanie and neighbouring tribes. Mieszko adopted Christianity – probably an astute political move to place the new state on equal footing with nearby Christian states with ties to Rome – and married a Czech princess, Dobrawa, in 965. His religious conversion won him the support of the papacy, and Mieszko effectively founded the Polish state the following year. By the end of the 10th century, he had united his tribal territory, Wielkopolska (Great Poland), with that of another tribe, Małopolska (Little Poland) – regional names that remain in use today. Silesia, settled by a different tribe, would eventually become the third component of the nascent Polish state.

Stained-glass window, Franciscan Church, Kraków

Mieszko's son Bolesław 'The Brave' was acknowledged by Otto III, the Holy Roman Emperor. Bolesław later repelled invasions from Otto's successor and then sought Poland's own expansion eastwards; he eventually annexed parts of present-day Ukraine. The Pope recognised Bolesław as the first king of Poland in 1025, elevating the country to full membership in a European community of Christian states.

Inbetween several often short, troubled and feuding reigns, Kazimierz I 'the Restorer' put the country on a firm footing again and established his court in Kraków. Kraków grew in importance and became the country's capital, replacing Gniezno in 1038. Kraków was better positioned for trade and also less vulnerable to attacks from the Czechs and Germans. Helped by the arrival of immigrants from all over Europe, including thousands of Jews, Kraków became a prosperous and culturally enriched capital.

From the mid-13th century, Tartars invaded Poland on three occasions. Threatened by the Prussians, Duke Konrad of Mazovia invited in the Order of the Teutonic Knights to help defend against them. The Knights used their considerable military might to then assume control of the very territory they had helped defend, capturing Gdańsk, securing most of the Baltic region and cutting off the rest of Poland from access to the sea. The Tartars defeated the Poles at the Battle of Legnica in 1241 and destroyed most of Kraków, leaving only the castle and St Andrew's Church intact.

KAZIMIERZ THE GREAT AND THE JAGIELLONIANS

The last king of the Piast dynasty, Kazimierz III, the Great, succeeded in reunifying Poland. His rule ushered in Poland's

THE TEUTONIC KNIGHTS

The Teutonic Knights were a military order of German knights who served in the Holy Land. They played an important part in Polish history, originally acquiring their prosperity through gifts of land for their hospital work during the Crusades. They were also given land in northeast Poland in 1225 in return for assisting the Mazovian Duke Konrad to repel an invasion of pagan Prussians. After annexing this Prussian territory, they gradually extended their occupation, invading Polish towns such as Gdańsk in the early 14th century and slaughtering the inhabitants, until their incursions were finally repulsed by the joint Polish-Lithuanian Commonwealth, and the knights were defeated in 1410 at the Battle of Grunwald. Malbork Castle (see page 103), established as the headquarters of the Knights' grand master, was taken over by the Poles in 1457 and the grand master swore allegiance to the Polish king.

first golden age. Kazimierz built great castles and towns, codified laws, and created an entire administrative system of governance for the war-torn country. He rebuilt Kraków with magnificent architecture and established the country's first university there. Kazimierz, a pragmatist, did not try to wrest control of Silesia, in the hands of Bohemia, or the territory seized by the independent state of the Teutonic Knights. Instead, he consolidated the state by expanding eastwards and accepting minority populations, including

Malbork Castle

persecuted Jews from across Europe, into the predominantly Catholic nation.

Kazimierz's death in 1370 left the crown to his nephew, Louis of Anjou, the King of Hungary. One of his daughters, Jadwiga, succeeded Louis in Poland, while the other assumed control of Hungary. Jadwiga's 1385 marriage to Władysław Jagiełło, the Grand Duke of Lithuania, led to Poland's strategic alliance with that powerful country. Following his wife's death, Jagiełło ruled both Poland and Lithuania for just shy of half a century, establishing a dynasty that would remain in power until 1572. The united countries defeated the Teutonic Knights at the Battle of Grunwald in 1410, halfway between Warsaw and the Lithuanian border, and repelled Germanic eastward expansion. The Thirteen

Battle of Grunwald, Jan Matejko

Years' War yielded great benefits for Poland: the transformation of Danzig (Gdańsk) into an independent city-state under the protection of the Polish crown and the capture of other Knights' territories.

Polish nobles saw their political might expand in the early Renaissance with the king's 'rule of the nobility', which granted exclusive right to enact legislation to nobles in the parliament, or Sejm. The 1500s saw prosperity, power and cultural and scientific achievement for the Polish-Lithuanian Commonwealth. Just before his death in 1543 Mikołaj Kopernik (Nicolaus Copernicus), born in Toruń and a graduate of the Jagiellonian University in Kraków, published his groundbreaking treatise, *De Revolutionibus Orbium Coeliestium*, which stated that the sun and not the earth is the centre of the universe. Although the Reformation and Lutherism had an impact on Poland, the country largely avoided the devastating religious wars that raged elsewhere in Europe.

The Sejm moved to Warsaw in 1529, and the death of the last ruler of the Jagiellonian dynasty, Zygmunt August, led to the creation of a Republic of Nobles and an elective monarchy that would serve it. Warsaw, better located in the centre of the country, became the official capital in 1596. King Zygmunt Waza (Sigismund Vasa) moved there from Kraków in 1609.

SWEDISH DYNASTY

Three successive elected kings emerged from the Swedish Waza dynasty. Sweden had become the strongest military power in Europe after the Thirty Years' War and in the mid-17th century the country set its expansionist sights on Poland. The Swedes invaded Poland in 1648, an event labelled the Swedish Deluge in Polish history books. The devastating war lasted five years, during which time Sweden was able to capture most of Poland. The war and the disastrous effects of the plague decimated the population of Poland, reducing it to just 4 million, roughly half its total in the early 17th century.

Remarkably, Poland retained enough military might to repel the Ottoman Turks in their advance through the Balkans. The military leader Jan Sobieski defeated Turkish troops at the Battle of Chocim in 1673, and Sobieski would later be credited with saving Vienna from Turkish forces . Sobieski was elected king of Poland in 1674, but his attention to battles against the Turks at the expense of domestic affairs did not bode well for him and Poland.

DECLINE AND PARTITIONING

At the start of the 18th century, Poland entered a prolonged period of decline, marked by financial ruin, a debilitated army, and a series of ineffectual kings. Poland was transformed into a client state of the Russians, and then lost much of its western territory to the Prussians during the Silesian Wars that ended in 1763. The following year Stanisław August Poniatowski was elected the last king of the Polish-Lithuanian Commonwealth, and Poland soon faced one of its most humiliating episodes.

The powerful Prussians came up with a plan to partition Poland, which gained the support of the Russians. The imposed treaty in 1772 robbed Poland of nearly a third of its lands. Yet Poniatowski recovered to preside over a reform movement that precipitated the creation of the 1791 Constitution, which restored the hereditary monarchy and overhauled Poland's political system. The liberal constitution, the oldest in the modern world after that of the United States, provided for the separation of powers among legislative, judicial and executive branches of the government.

None of these reforms pleased the Russians and Prussians, who continued to covet Polish territory. Russia invaded Poland and in 1792–3 it, along with Prussia, imposed a second partition of Poland, annulling the constitution and essentially divvying up the country between them. Tadeusz Kościuszko, a hero of the American War of Independence, led a military insurrection in 1794, defeating the Russians with a mostly peasant army. The uprising was quashed, however, and in 1795, Poniatowski was forced to abdicate. A third partition crushed Poland and placed the country under the control of Austria, Prussia and Russia. Poland ceased to exist for the next 123 years. Warsaw went to Prussia, Kraków to the mighty Austrian empire.

In desperation, Poland looked to Napoleon Bonaparte and Revolutionary France for assistance against its oppressors. Napoleon defeated the Prussian army in several key battles and established a semi-independent Duchy of Warsaw from 1807 to 1815. Napoleon gained an ally in Józef Poniatowski, a heralded military leader and the nephew of the last king. The 1812 Polish War re-established the Poland–Lithuania border, but Napoleon's troops were crushed as they advanced on Moscow. Napoleon suffered a great defeat, but his ally Poniatowski refused to surrender, preferring to sacrifice himself and his troops. The suicidal mission became an important rallying cry for Poles during the remainder of the 19th century.

The Congress of Vienna of 1815, which aimed to reorganise Europe after the Napoleonic Wars, did not re-establish an independent Poland. Rather, it re-partitioned the country, placing the Duchy of Warsaw under the control of the Russian tsar. For three decades, Kraków existed as an independent city-state, though it was incorporated into the Austrian partition in 1846.

The former Duchy of Warsaw, called the Congress Kingdom, enjoyed some autonomy and prosperity in the early 19th century. Poles launched a series of armed insurrections against its occupiers in 1830 and, after defeat, again in 1846 and 1863. Many Poles emigrated to France and then the United States during this period. Those who remained focused on preserving Polish language and culture, if not the Polish state.

THE AFTERMATH OF WORLD WAR I

The next pivotal episode in Polish history coincided with the end of World War I and the defeat of the Russians, Germans and Austrians. The partition of Poland collapsed in 1918, and Poland's bid for independence won the support of both

The Cossack massacre during the January Uprising, 1863

Pianist and PM

In 1918 the acclaimed concert pianist, Ignacy Jan Paderewski (1860–1941), served as one of the Polish Republic's first prime ministers, signing the Treaty of Versailles on behalf of his country. He later lived in exile in the United States.

American president Woodrow Wilson and the Bolshevik government in Russia. The Polish war hero Józef Piłsudski (1867–1935), released from a German prison, took control of Poland. In 1920, the Soviets invaded, but Piłsudski and his troops managed to stop the advance at the Vistula and went on to occupy parts of Ukraine and Lithuania.

In 1926, Piłsudski engineered a military coup and seized control under the Sanacja, or sanation, government that would rule until the start of World War II. By 1933, Poland was sandwiched between two dictatorships: Stalin in Russia on the eastern border, and Hitler in Nazi Germany to the west. Both fixed their eyes on occupying Poland, and they signed the ruthless Nazi–Soviet Pact on 23 August 1939, which stated that either would be free to pursue expansionist acts without the interference of the other. In the agreement was a secret clause providing for the eventual full partition of Poland between Germany and Russia – even though Poland had signed 10-year non-aggression pacts with both.

NAZI INVASION, WORLD WAR II AND THE HOLOCAUST

On 1 September 1939, the Nazis invaded Poland. The annexation of Danzig (modern day Gdańsk) marked the official start of World War II. Soon after, German forces launched an occupation of Kraków, where they based their governing body, and laid siege to Warsaw. The Soviets invaded Poland less than two weeks later on 17 September, following the terms of the pact signed with Germany.

The Nazis initiated a ruthless campaign in 1940, rounding up intellectuals, Jews and others, executing some in the streets and deporting others to concentration camps in the occupied territory. Craftsmen and labourers were deported to do forced labour in the Reich. Artists, scientists and priests were taken into 'protective custody', which was often a synonym for concentration camps. The Germans constructed walled Jewish ghettoes in Warsaw and Kraków. At death camps such as Auschwitz (see page 60), near Kraków, the Nazis eventually murdered millions of Poles and Jews, as well as other prisoners from across Europe. The Soviets themselves imprisoned some 1.5 million Poles in labour camps of their own and eliminated potential 'troublemakers' through actions like the Katyn massacre in 1940, in which more than 20,000 Polish military officers and civilians were summarily executed.

From 1941–5 Poland was under Nazi occupation, and the

The Wehrmacht parade down Ujazdów Avenue, Warsaw

country became the focus of Hitler's campaign to exterminate Jews and non-Aryans. Hitler invaded the Soviet Union in 1941, an act that drew the Soviets and Poles together in a shaky alliance.

A heroic uprising in 1943, led by poorly armed Jews in the Warsaw ghetto, lasted a month until Nazi reinforcements annihilated it and reported back to Germany that 'Warsaw's Jewish quarter has ceased to exist'. The following year, Poland's Home Army initiated a surprise attack against the occupying Nazis in Warsaw, and awaited assistance from the Soviet Red Army, perched on the outskirts of the capital. The military support never came, and as his troops left the city after quashing the insurgency, Hitler ordered them to raze Warsaw building by building and thereby annihilate important monuments of Polish culture. When the Soviets entered the city, they found it reduced to rubble and ashes.

World War II was more devastating for Poland than any other country. Six million Poles lost their lives during World War II, and the Jewish population was reduced from three million to just a couple of thousand. Poland lost a significant amount of territory after new borders were drawn up in the Yalta Agreement of February 1945, including the eastern regions around Wilno (Vilnius) and Lwów (Lvov). The Polish borders shifted west a couple of hundred kilometres, incorporating ancient parts of Silesia such as Wrocław, the pre-war German city of Breslau. Poland also regained Danzig, not a part of Poland since its seizure by the Teutonic Knights. The city reverted to its original Polish name, Gdańsk.

COMMUNISM AND SOVIET DOMINATION

In the aftermath of the war, Poland was Sovietised, with the installation of a Soviet-friendly communist regime, the nationalisation of businesses, confiscation of church property, and forced exile of political and religious leaders. With Soviet aid, a rebuilding programme was initiated, an effort that reconstructed the Old Towns of Warsaw and Gdańsk, among others, in costly and meticulous efforts based on paintings, photographs and architectural drawings. The Soviet Union signalled its domination over Poland with the 1955 'gift' of the Palace of Culture and Science in Warsaw, a towering skyscraper that would become a hated symbol of foreign influence.

Monument to the Warsaw Uprising, Warsaw

Many Poles, especially among the intellectual and professional classes, opposed Soviet influence and Communist rule, and in 1956 the regime faced its first real test. Worker strikes and protests erupted in Poznań, and spread into armed confrontations in the streets. Security forces opened fire on rioters and killed scores of people, including a 13 year-old boy. A weakened and suddenly unstable Communist Party installed former First Secretary Gomułka as leader. The episode in Poland, known as the Polish October, exposed cracks in the Communist regime, and served as the impetus for a slight relaxation of censorship, religious repression and economic controls. Reforms stalled, however, and the following decade saw a return to strict Soviet doctrine. The 1970s were marked by inflation, strikes and protests. Living standards dropped dramatically, and the Soviet Union was forced to prop up the Polish economy.

POPE JOHN PAUL II AND SOLIDARITY

In 1978, the Polish Cardinal and Archbishop of Kraków Karol Wojtyła was elected Pope; he took the name John Paul II. A staunch opponent of the Communist regime, Wojtyła returned to Poland from Rome in 1979 as Pope and drew great, joyful crowds at every stop. The following year, unrest grew among workers after massive increases in food prices. Lech Wałęsa, a shipyard electrician, led strikes in Gdańsk. The size and vehemence of their protests, which spread countrywide, forced the government to negotiate with the Solidarność (Solidarity) trade union, granting its workers' demands and allowing free trade unions limited autonomy to oversee their industries. With hindsight, Solidarity was critical in establishing the foundations for opposition to Communist rule across Central and Eastern Europe.

General Wojciech Jaruzelski adopted a hard line and declared martial law in December 1981 in response to continued strikes across Poland. Thousands of Solidarity activists and sympathisers were arrested, the trade union banned while the civil rights

CATHOLIC RESISTANCE

The Roman Catholic Church was one of the few institutions that retained a level of independence in Communist Poland, a fact that led to Stalin's celebrated remark comparing imposing Communism on the Poles to putting a saddle on a cow. The Communists did their best however, regarding the Church as a reactionary relic of the pre-war system. Repression was severe: priests and laymen alike were openly attacked and constantly threatened with arrest by the government, and by 1950 the financial assets of the Church had been confiscated. In 1953, one of the heroes of this frightening era, Cardinal Stefan Wyszyński, the primate of Poland, was arrested for his anti-state attitudes. He was exiled to a monastery where he was held prisoner for three years.

suspended. Two years later, the regime lifted martial law after the Pope John Paul's second visit to Poland, and Lech Wałęsa won the Nobel Peace Prize in 1983, familiarising the world with the struggles of Polish workers.

The government's resolve did not waver, however. In 1984, the Polish secret police murdered Father Jerzy Popiełuszko, an outspoken supporter of Solidarność.

The mid-1980s witnessed a gradual programme of liberalisation in Poland on the heels of Mikhail Gorbachev's perestroika and glasnost in

Palace of Culture, Warsaw

the Soviet Union, the promises of greater openness and economic freedoms. In 1989, talks established the basis for limited power sharing between the Communist Party and Solidarity.

THE END OF COMMUNIST RULE

Desperate austerity measures failed to jump-start the economy. In semi-free elections, Solidarity was the overwhelming victor, and the Communist regime collapsed. On 9 December 1990, Poles made Lech Wałęsa the first popularly elected president in post-World War II Poland. The following year, the Warsaw Pact was dissolved.

Poland's road to capitalism and democracy has been a complicated one. Wałęsa fell out of favour with Poles and was defeated in the 1995 elections. But by that time, the country

Polish Parliament in session

had joined the World Trade Organization, and the EU had agreed to open negotiations to admit Poland.

Poland joined NATO in 1999 and the EU five years later. Huge crowds turned out for every one of John Paul II's many visits to his homeland up to and including his last visit in 2002, and his death in 2005 was widely mourned; both signs that Poland's committed Catholics and fervent patriots had survived Communism with their faith and pride intact. The country was rocked in April 2010, when the serving president Lech Kaczyński and his wife, former president Ryszard Kaczorowski and many important people in Polish politics, business and the military, were among the 96 passengers on board the plane that crashed near Smolensk. There were no survivors. They were on their way to mark the 70th anniversary of the massacre at Katyn. The following year Poland assumed presidency of the European Union for the first time.

The eight-year rule (2007-2015) of the centre right Democratic Platform (PO) led by Donald Tusk saw unprecedented economic growth in Poland which did not succumb to the 2008 crisis. A massive influx of EU funds as well as hosting of the Euro 2012 football championships triggered a massive road construction and modernisation plan. However, a series of corruption scandals as well as failure to implement the long overdue reforms undermined PO's popularity. As a result, the right wing Law and Justice (PiS) scored a historic double victory: first in the presidential and then in the parliamentary elections held in 2015.

HISTORICAL LANDMARKS

966 The founding of Poland.

992 Bolesław I Chrobry (the Brave) is crowned first king of Poland.

1309 The Teutonic Order rules over a large territory along the Eastern Baltic Sea, including Gdańsk.

1325 Polish-Lithuanian alliance formed against the Teutonic Knights.

1333 Kazimierz III Wielki doubles the size of his realm, expanding to the east and transforming Poland into a multinational state.

1364 Founding of Kraków University.

1386 Founding of the Jagiellonian dynasty.

1410 Teutonic Knights are defeated at the Battle of Grunwald; Poland becomes a more powerful, unified realm.

1543 Copernicus publishes *De Revolutionibus Orbium Coelestium*.

1569 Poland and Lithuania are united into a single Commonwealth.

1655–60 Sweden invades Poland.

1673 Jan Sobieski defeats the Turks at the Battle of Chocim.

1772, 93-95 Poland divided among Prussia, Austria and Russia.

1918 Independent Polish state created after the end of World War I.

1939 German troops invade Poland, triggering World War II.

1943 Warsaw Ghetto Uprising.

1944 Warsaw Uprising by Polish Home Army; city is razed by the Nazis.

1945 After the end of World War II, new borders are established by the victorious Allies. The Communists take power.

1981 Martial law is proclaimed after disturbances spearheaded by the trade union Solidarity (Solidarność), led by Lech Wałęsa.

1989 Roundtable talks between the union Solidarność (Solidarity) the Communists and the Catholic Church.

1990 Lech Wałęsa wins the presidential election.

1999 Poland becomes a member of NATO.

2004 Poland joins the European Union (EU).

2005 Polish-born Pope John Paul II dies.

2010 President Kaczyński among 96 dead in Smolensk plane crash.

2015 The right wing Law and Justice (PiS) wins presidential and parliamentary elections.

WHERE TO GO

Poland, bordering the Baltic Sea to the north, Germany to the west, the Czech Republic and Slovakia to the south, and Ukraine, Belarus, Lithuania and Russia to the east, is large and predominantly rural. The main points of interest for first-time visitors are the principal cities, beginning with Kraków, Warsaw and Gdańsk – whose old towns certainly rank among the finest of Central Europe, and smaller, well-preserved towns that are rich in history, architecture and Polish character. It is also a place to see great castles, memorials of Jewish culture that mark unspeakable tragedy, and churches and synagogues that are sites of important Catholic and Jewish pilgrimage.

It's easy and inexpensive to get around Poland by train, probably the preferred method of navigating the country. Exploring the Polish countryside requires either a lot of time and patience, or a car. And even one's personal transport can be sometimes be slow-going, as the Polish road system outside of the big cities has lagged behind the country's speedy development in other areas. That said, new cross-country highways are making a big difference. For visitors with plenty of time, the mountains, sea and lake districts have much to offer, although this guide deals primarily with the major Polish cities and towns.

Because Kraków is the country's most popular tourist destination, this section begins there, in southeast Poland. Just beyond Kraków, reached in easy day trips, are the fantastic 700-year-old Wieliczka salt mines and the horrendous physical legacy of the Nazi concentration camps of Auschwitz. In southern Poland, along the Slovakian border, are the Tatra Mountains and the delightful ski resort town of Zakopane. To the southeast of the country, between Kraków and Ukraine, is the 16th-century Renaissance town Zamość. Almost in the

St Mary's Basilica on Kraków's Rynek Główny (Main Market Square)

Adolf Hitler Platz

When Kraków was occupied by the Nazis, the Main Market Square was renamed Adolf Hitler Platz.

exact geographical centre of Poland is the present-day capital and commercial centre, Warsaw. Nearby is Łódź, Poland's third city. In north and northwest Poland are Gdańsk on the Baltic Sea, and nearby Malbork Castle, the most splendid fortification in Poland and the largest brick castle in the world. Toruń was the birthplace of the great Polish astronomer Copernicus, while Poznań is one of the most ancient centres in Poland and today one of its most dynamic cities.

KRAKOW

Elegant **Kraków** ❶, the former royal capital of Poland, is one of the finest old cities in Europe. More than a thousand years old, and the country's capital for half that time, Kraków is Poland's second-largest city, with 760,000 residents, plus some 100,000 students. It is also considered the heart and soul of Poland, home to many of its greatest artists, writers, musicians, filmmakers and one of the world's oldest universities. It is one of the few major towns in Poland not devastated by the world wars of the 20th century, and its miraculously preserved medieval market square and castle make it Poland's most seductive city.

Though awe-inspiring churches, monuments and museums line its ancient streets, and the historic royal castle overlooks the Old Town from a hilltop, Kraków is one of Poland's liveliest and hippest cities. It abounds with young, fashionable café-hoppers. Kraków's roster of bars and cafés, many of them idiosyncratic places in underground cellars, are among the city's undeniable highlights. Almost everything of interest in Kraków is easily managed on foot, with the possible exception of Kazimierz, the old Jewish quarter that lies just south of the Old Town.

MAIN MARKET SQUARE AND OLD TOWN

Kraków's layout dates from 1257 and remains almost unchanged to this day. The streets are lined with historic townhouses, fine churches and delightful small shops. The whole of the largely pedestrianised Old Town (Stare Miasto) is encircled by the **Planty**, a ring of relaxing parklands where massive fortifications and a wide moat once protected the city. The best place to begin to get to know Kraków is Europe's largest medieval Market Square, **Rynek Główny Ⓐ**, at the heart of the Old Town. The spectacular square pulsates with youthful energy at all hours, and its pavement cafés are fine places to enjoy the pleasant surroundings, people watch, and catch sight of traditional horse-drawn carriages. Many of the houses that line the square have Neo-Classical façades, though they are considerably older than that, and are full of interesting architectural details.

Eros Bendato sculpture, Kraków

At the centre of the square is the **Cloth Hall** (Sukiennice), built in the 14th century and reconstructed after a fire in 1555 in the Renaissance style (the arcades were added in the 19th century). The building once housed the richest of Kraków's cloth merchants, and today its ground-floor stalls are occupied by privileged sellers of amber jewellery, religious artefacts, art and souvenirs targeting Kraków's year-round tourist trade. Don't miss Rynek Underground, an excellent interactive museum – a branch of the Kraków Historical Museum (MHK; www.mhk.pl) – located in the cellars below the main square that presents Krakow's rich history as well as its connections with other European cultural and trading centres; and the Gallery of 19th century Polish Art (branch of the National Museum in Kraków; http://mnk.pl) on the upper floor of the Cloth Hall featuring paintings and sculptures by Polish masters includingWładysław Podkowiński, Józef Chełmoński, Jacek Malczewski and Aleksander Gierymski.

Next to the Cloth Hall is the 15th-century **Town Hall Tower**; the rest of the Town Hall was demolished in the early 19th century. Southeast of it is tiny **St Adalbert's Church** (Kościół Św. Wojciecha). Intriguingly, the copper-domed 11th-century church is a few steps down, showing the original level of the

ST MARY'S TRUMPETER

Every hour, a trumpeter appears in the tallest tower of St Mary's Basilica to play the Hejnał Mariacki, a call to arms that began as a warning of the advancing Tartar army in 1241. The tradition has been continued down the centuries ever since. The bugle call ends mid-bar, a symbol of the story that the lone watchman was felled by an arrow as he warned the city. Watch the trumpeter from the passageway just south of the church; at the end of the piece, he waves to those gathered below.

square. The branch of the **Kraków Historical Museum** (Rynek Główny 35)) in the former Krzysztofory Palace, presents permanent (Cyberteka) as well as temporary exhibitions including the wonderful Christmas cribs every December.

Sukiennice - the Cloth Hall, Kraków

ST MARY'S BASILICA

On the eastern side of the square, just beyond a statue of the 19th-century Romantic poet Adam Mickiewicz – a hangout for local youths and backpackers from around the globe – is **St Mary's Basilica** **B** (Kościół Mariacki; Mon–Sat 11.30am–6pm, Sun 2–6pm; www.mariacki. com). Its asymmetrical towers are one of Kraków's most celebrated images and the hejnał, or bugle call sounds hourly from the tallest tower, one of the city's iconic sounds. A church was founded on this spot in 1221–2, and it faced east, as was the custom of the day. St Mary's, built on the original foundations in the 14th century, also sits at an angle to the square.

The main entrance, a Baroque porch façade, is used only by those attending Mass. Tourists are asked to enter through the side door, through Plac Mariacki off Rynek Główny. Inside is a stunning kaleidoscope of ornamentation and colour, with extraordinary wall paintings by Jan Matejko in blue, green and pink. The ceiling of the main nave is painted a bold blue with gold stars. The highlight, set beneath five tall columns of stained-glass windows, is the sumptuous altarpiece, a masterwork of Polish Gothic that took the 15th-century German master carver Veit Stoss (Wit Stwosz) 12 years to create in linden wood. The powerful triptych shows the Dormition of the Virgin

Mary, flanked by scenes of the life of Christ and the Virgin. Over the central nave is a massive crucifix; at the rear of the church, behind the organ loft are fine examples of Art Nouveau stained glass, the work of Kraków's Stanisław Wyspiański.

The little courtyard south of St Mary's leads to **St Barbara's Church** (Kościół Św. Barbary) and a passageway onto **Little Market Square** (Mały Rynek), where colourful façades line what was once the marketplace of meat, fish and poultry vendors.

Leading north off the Main Market Square is ul. Floriańska, a busy pedestrian-only street full of shops, restaurants and cafés. On the eastern side is the **Jan Matejko House** (Dom Jana Matejki; Tue–Sat 10am–6pm, Sun 10am–4pm), the home where the influential 19th-century Polish artist was born, worked and died. It includes memorabilia and a number of paintings from his personal collection, and much of the house stands as the artist left it upon his death in 1893. At the end

Inside St Mary's Basilica

of the street, and the edge of the Old Town, is **Florian's Gate** **C** (Brama Floriańska), one of the original seven gates in the city's fortified walls. Built early in the 14th century, it is the only one to have survived 19th-century modernisation plans. An outdoor art market takes place here daily, and pictures executed in every conceivable style blanket the stone walls. The view down Floriańska towards the spire of St Mary's is one of the most priceless in Kraków.

Just beyond the gate is the **Barbican** **D** (Barbakan; Apr–Oct daily 10.30am–6pm; www.mhk.pl/branches/barbican), a circular brick bastion built at the end of the 15th century and one of the few remaining structures of the medieval fortifications. It was originally connected to the Floriańska Gate over a moat. Nearby are two buildings of significance. On the edge of the Planty to the southeast is the **Church of the Holy Cross** (Kościół Św. Krzyża; pl. Św. Ducha), a small 15th-century church with splendid Gothic vaulting; almost next to it is the eclectic **Słowacki Theatre** (Teatr im. Juliusza Słowackiego; pl. Św. Ducha 1; www. slowacki.krakow.pl), a bright yellow-and-green-roofed structure built in 1893 and modelled after the Paris Opera House. Don't miss the curious laughing gargoyles on the rooftop.

THE CZARTORYSKI AND WYSPIAŃSKI MUSEUMS

At the top of ul. Św. Jana, the street running parallel and to the west of Floriańska, is one of the Old Town's highlights – the **Czartoryski Museum** **E** (Muzeum Czartoryskich, currently a branch of the National Museum in Kraków). The main building of the museum is closed for restoration (scheduled for reopening in 2017), so the museum's most popular treasure – Leonardo da Vinci's Lady with an Ermine – is being temporarily displayed at Wawel Castle (although rumour has it that it might be moved yet again to the Arsenal building sometime in 2016). See the museums' websites (http://mnk.pl; http://muzeum.czartoryskich.pl)

for details. Meanwhile, the Czartoryski's Ancient Art Gallery with splendid examples of works from Greece, Eturia, Egypt and Rome can be seen at the Arsenal building across the street from the main building (Galerii Sztuki Starożytnej w Arsenale Książąt Czartoryskich; Tue–Sun 10am–4pm).

On Plac Szczepański (Szczepański square), adjacent to the edifices of the Stary Theatre and the Palace of Fine Art, is the Szołayski House, another branch of the National Museum, featuring permanent and temporary exhibitions as well as hosting lectures, concerts and art lessons for children and young adults. The ground floor of the renovated building houses an information centre, a museum shop, a café and a multipurpose hall. It previously housed the Stanisław Wyspiański Museum commemorating the great 19th century Kraków artist (the collection is currently undergoing restoration works).

Rembrant's Landscape with the good Samaritan, one of the masterpieces from the Czartoryski collection.

Wyspiański is perhaps best known for his stained glass and decorative frescoes (as seen in St Francis' Basilica; see page 42), but he was also a poet, designer and dramatist.

JAGIELLONIAN UNIVERSITY

The area south and west of the main market square is home to the famed **Jagiellonian University**, the oldest university in Poland and one of the oldest in Europe, and several fine churches. Take any of the streets heading west from the square, such as Św. Anny. Enter a small door beneath the Flemish-style roof to the **Collegium Maius ⊙**, the oldest building of the university and a beautiful 15th-century Gothic structure with an arcaded central courtyard. Notice the fanciful drainage pipe heads, of medieval dragons and the like, on the rooftop. King Kazimierz established the university in 1364, but its golden age dates to the period of the reign of King Jagiełło, for whom it is named. Copernicus allegedly studied here in the 15th century.

Here you will find the **Jagiellonian University Museum** (Muzeum Uniwersytetu Jagiellońskiego; Mon–Sat 10am–2.20pm, till 5.20pm on Tue andThu in Apr–Oct; times vary for English language tours; advance booking recommended, tel: 012 663 15 21; www.maius.uj.edu.pl). On the guided visit through the ornate academic halls, the treasury, library and professors' dining hall – you can see several objects related to the university's most famous collegian and his theory that revolutionised our notion of the universe, including astronomical instruments, a registrar's book signed 'Mikołaj Kopernik', and a very rare globe, dating back to 1520, with the earliest known depiction of the Americas. Pope John Paul II was once an undergraduate at this university, and Poland's most recent Nobel Prize winner for literature, the late Wisława Szymborska, donated her medal and a good portion of the prize to the museum.

A tour group at Collegium Maius

OLD TOWN CHURCHES

The streets near here are always filled with students – Kraków has nearly 100,000 students attending the university's 12 colleges and academic institutes. Around the corner from the Collegium Maius is **St Anne's Church** (Kościół Św. Anny; ul. Św. Anny 11), linked to the university and a favourite location for students getting married. The 17th-century interior is a superb example of airy Polish Baroque, with a high dome, spectacular stucco work and wall murals. Facing the Planty is the **Collegium Novum**, a late 19th-century neo-Gothic building decorated with the crests of the university and its most celebrated benefactors. When Hitler's troops invaded Kraków in 1939, they stormed this hall and arrested nearly 200 professors and academics, and hauled them off to concentration camps.

On ul. Franciszkańska, directly south of the market square, is the unmissable **St Francis' Basilica ❻** (Kościół Św. Franciszka z Asyżu; pl. Wszystkich Świętych), dating from 1269. The gutted interior was rebuilt in the 19th century after

MAIN MARKET SQUARE AND OLD TOWN

the last of four disastrous fires. Relatively unassuming from the exterior, the exuberant interior is a stunning assembly of brilliant stained glass and colourful wall paintings in floral and geometric motifs. At the rear above the organ loft is a remarkable Art Nouveau stained-glass window designed by the local artist Stanisław Wyspiański, a disciple of Jan Matejko, in 1900. The large 'Act of Creation' depicts God in wild streaks of colour. Wyspiański reportedly based God's face on the countenance of a beggar. The stained-glass windows behind the altar, also by Wyspiański, depict the Blessed Salomea to the left and St Francis to the right. To the right of the altar is a passage to the Gothic cloister with its 15th-century frescoes and portraits of the bishops of Kraków. The painting at the end of the hall is of the 'lady who stopped the fire', a reference to the great fire of 1850 that was miraculously snuffed out at that very wall of the Franciscan church.

East of here the street changes name in honour of another religious order and its 13th-century church, the **Dominican Church and Monastery** (Kościół Dominikanów; ul. Stolarska 12). It too suffered from fire damage, and today is notable for its neo-Gothic chapels and original 15th-century portal. The monastery has serene Gothic cloisters.

Heading south towards Wawel Hill, along ul. Grodzka, is **SS Peter and Paul's Church ⓗ** (Kościół Św. Piotra i Św. Pawła; ul. Grodzka 54), recognised by its large dome and long row of stately statues of the Twelve Apostles out front. The oldest Baroque building in Kraków, the basilica was founded by the Jesuits in the early 1600s. The rather austere late-Renaissance interior has recently been renovated.

The small Romanesque church next door is **St Andrew's** (Kościół Św. Andrzeja;

City of churches

Kraków is said to have in excess of 125 churches – 60 of them in the Old Town alone.

Sculptures in front of SS Peter and Paul's Church

ul. Grodzka 56), dating from the 11th century and one of the oldest churches in Kraków. Its colourful history includes a stint as a hiding place and fortress for Poles battling invading Tartars in 1241.

Across the square facing those two churches, turn down ul. Kanonicza, one of Kraków's oldest and most attractive streets. On the way to Wawel Hill, at ul. Kanonicza 9, is the house where Stanisław Wyspiański lived and worked in the early 20th century.

Down the street, at ul. Kanonicza 19, is the **Archdiocesan Museum ❶** (Muzeum Archidiecezjalne; ul. Kanonicza 19; Tue–Fri 10am–4pm, Sat–Sun 10am–3pm; www.muzeum kra.diecezja.pl), where Pope John Paul II lived on two occasions, first as a young priest and then as Bishop of Kraków. The neighbouring 14th-century houses now contain a small museum of notable 13th- to 20th-century religious art, including a collection of Gothic sculptures of the Madonna and child, and artefacts belonging to the Pope, including the room where he lived (with his desk, bed and two pairs of skis), photographs, and ornate gifts from heads of state and religious leaders.

The other buildings on ul. Kanonicza are also worth a closer look, as many are former palaces with a range of architectural features, including Gothic, Renaissance and Baroque. The beautifully restored Ciołek Palace (Pałac Ciołka) at Kanonicza 17 built between 1501 and 1503 now houses a branch of the Kraków National Museum including some priceless Orthodox icons and a gallery of Polish art from the 12th to 18th centuries. Continuing along ul. Kanonicza, past the exclusive Hotel Copernicus, leads you towards Wawel Hill.

WAWEL HILL

A castle or royal palace has existed on Wawel Hill overlooking the Old Town of Kraków since the 9th century, though the area may have been inhabited as early as the Paleolithic Age. The first kings of Poland maintained a royal residence here from the 10th century until King Zygmunt Waza (Sigismund Vasa) moved the royal seat to Warsaw in 1596. Over the centuries the castle was repeatedly destroyed by invaders and war, ultimately transformed into the complex that today is a mix of Gothic, Renaissance, Baroque and neo-Classical architecture.

Wawel, a symbol of the Polish nation, is a great source of national pride to Poles, and it is a popular place of spiritual pilgrimage.

Ticket tips

Separate tickets are needed for the cathedral and castle complexes. Guided group visits are available at the main box office past the cathedral (there are two other box offices, including one on the path on the way up the hill). The various component parts of Wawel have different opening hours, so be sure to check them before visiting. For the latest information, check the official Wawel website at www.wawel.krakow.pl.

The most popular sites to visit are the royal castle and chambers, treasury and armoury, the cathedral and royal tombs, and Sigismund stairs to the bell tower. Expect crowds, especially in summer, and allow at least half a day for a visit.

THE CATHEDRAL

The Gothic edifice of **Wawel Cathedral ❶** (Katedra; Apr–Sept Mon–Sat 9am–5pm, Sun 12.30–5pm; Oct–Mar Mon–Sat 9am–4pm, Sun 12.30pm–4pm Cathedral Museum closed Sun; Cathedral free; charge only for the crypt, bell tower and Museum; www.katedra-wawelska.pl) – the third cathedral built on this site – was begun in 1320, some three centuries after the first. The site of half a millennium of royal coronations and burials, it is the final resting place of nearly all the kings of Poland. The entrance is marked by a set of very large bones – those of a prehistoric woolly rhinoceros – found on the site.

Inside Wawel Cathedral

At the centre of the nave is an ornate **shrine to St Stanislaus** (św Stanisław), the 13th-century bishop of Kraków who was martyred by the Polish king Bolesław in 1079. The saint's body was dismembered but, according to legend, it became whole again – a sign taken as a portent that a divided Poland, partitioned by Germany, Russia and Austria, would also reunify itself. The cathedral witnessed the coronation of 32 kings, each of whom knelt before the shrine and asked St Stanislaus for forgiveness. Of particular interest among the various tombs, altars and chapels is the Renaissance-style **Sigismund Chapel**, designed by the Italian architect Bartolomeo Berrecci (it's the one with the golden dome). To the right of the entrance, the **Holy Cross Chapel** is a feast of 14th-century Byzantine frescoes and the late 15th-century marble sarcophagus of King Casimir IV Jagiełło, which was carved in reddish marble by Veit Stoss.

The steep, wooden 14th-century stairs leading to the **Sigismund Belltower** are not for the claustrophobic or disabled, but for the athletically inclined. They are a fun climb up to see the revered Zygmunt bell, which dates to the mid-16th century and is the largest bell in Poland, requiring eight people to ring it. Krakovians say they can hear the bell from as far as 20km (12 miles) away when it is rung on major holidays.

Next to the altar is the tomb of Kazimierz the Great, the so-called 'Builder of Poland'. The sepulchres of the Sigismund kings, the beloved Queen Jadwiga and others lie in the main body of the cathedral, while below in the **Royal Crypts** are the tombs of 10 Polish kings and their families, as well as a handful of national military and literary heroes, including Marshal Piłsudski, who has a small and decidedly atmospheric crypt all to himself. Controversially, in 2010, Poland's President Lech Kaczyński joined their number after dying in the Smolensk plane crash. The entrance to the tombs is towards the back of the church, and the exit is onto the main castle courtyard.

Wawel Castle

CASTLE HIGHLIGHTS

Wawel Castle , also an enduring symbol of Polish nationhood, was the royal residence until the capital moved to Warsaw in 1596. King Bolesław built the first and considerably smaller residence in the 11th century, but it became a grand, Gothic palace during the reign of Kazimierz the Great in the 14th century. A great fire razed it in 1499, and the elegant Renaissance palace that was rebuilt by King Zygmunt the Old is largely the structure one sees today. Swedes, Prussians and Austrians all overran and occupied the castle and its grounds at different times, and the last group of invaders destroyed churches and built military barracks, leaving the hill with an oddly empty square and large and plainer buildings to the west of the castle. The Polish government and people did not recover Wawel until the end of World War I in 1918, when the partition of Poland ended.

Visitor numbers on the hill are restricted, and entry to some of the sights is by timed ticket only. To reserve in advance tel: 012 422 51 55 ext. 219 or 012 422 16 97. Collect reserved tickets at the Tourist Service Office (Biuro Obsługi Turystów), inside the square near the entrance to the arcaded courtyard at least 20 minutes before the reserved time, or from the ticket offices at Herbowa Gate (Brama Herbowa) or Bernadyńska Gate. You can also reserve timed tickets at these ticket offices. See www.wawel.krakow.pl.

The **State Rooms** and **Royal Private Apartments** (Reprezentacyjne Komnaty Królewskie and Prywatne Apartamenty Królewskie; Apr–Oct Tue–Fri 9.30am–5pm, Sat–Sun 10am–4pm; Nov–Mar Tue–Sat 9.30am–4pm, Sat–Sun 10am–4pm, Royal Private Apartments closed Sun in winter; State Rooms free Sun Dec–Mar; admission to Royal Private Apartments in groups of up to 10, guided tours only, fee includes guide) are the largest and most interesting part of the castle. They have been restored to their original Renaissance style and furnished with Baroque and Renaissance furniture (much of which is not original to the castle). The most impressive and valuable items on display are the spectacular collection of 16th-century Flemish tapestries commissioned by King Sigismund. Only 136 of the original 364 tapestries survive, and not all are on view. Also on view is a handsome collection of 17th-century Turkish tents.

Don't miss the opportunity to see the priceless Leonardo da Vinci's *Lady with an Ermine* (same opening hours as the Royal Apartments and State Rooms) that belongs to the Czartoryski Museum (currently under renovation) and is being temporarily displayed at Wawel. It is one of only three da Vinci oil canvases left in the world.

The **Deputies Hall**, or Throne Room, is also called the 'Room of Heads', a name that is explained once you glance at the ceiling. It is studded with small carved wooden heads of some 30 citizens of Renaissance-period Kraków – ordinary folk, not just royalty, nobles and clergy as might be expected. Over the king's throne is a stunning Flemish tapestry. The **Senators' Room** is tapestried wall-to-wall, with tapestries placed over the windows, reportedly so there would be no outside distractions during important Senate sessions.

The **Treasury and Armoury** (Skarbiec Koronny i Zbrojownia; Apr–Oct Mon 9.30am–1pm, Tue–Fri 9.30am–5pm, Sat–Sun 10am–5pm; Nov–Mar Tue–Sat 9.30am–4pm, closed Mon–Sun; free Mon Apr–Oct), house the royal collection of weaponry and spoils of war, including the 13th-century Szczerbiec, a Royal jagged sword used at all Polish coronations.

Lost Wawel is an exhibition, across the garden from the cathedral, housed within the former royal kitchens and coach house (Wawel Zaginiony; Apr–Oct Mon 9.30am–1pm, Tue–Fri 9.30am–5pm, Sat–Sun 10am–5pm; Nov–Mar Tue–Sat 9.30am–4pm, Sun 10am–4pm, free Mon Apr–Oct Sun Nov–Mar) in which some fascinating archaeological and architectural remains are on display,

At the far end of the castle grounds, (walk towards the Baszta Sandomierska exit) you will find Wawel's **Dragon's Cave** (Smocza Jama; daily Apr, Sept, Oct 10am–5pm; May–June 10am–6pm; July–Aug 10am–7pm; Nov–Mar closed; charge), according to legend the home of a reclusive dragon, Smok Wawelski. From here you emerge on the banks of the Vistula River.

KAZIMIERZ

Once the old Jewish district of Kraków, **Kazimierz** ❶ was originally built in 1335 as an independent, planned and walled town by the Polish king whose name it took. Jews, persecuted throughout Europe, were offered refuge all over Kraków, but King Jan Olbracht moved Kraków's entire Jewish population to Kazimierz at the end of the 15th century. Today the district is essentially a suburb within easy walking distance or a short tram or taxi ride from the Old Town.

Before the war, some 60,000 Jews lived in the Kraków area. Only a few thousand remained in 1945, and today there are reportedly as few as 200 here. After decades of neglect, having been robbed of its people and soul – although many of its buildings survived the war – Kazimierz is undergoing a revitalisation.

Jewish foundations from around the world are funding the restoration of historic buildings, and Steven Spielberg brought new attention to Kazimierz with his Academy Award-winning 1994 film *Schindler's List*, though only a few scenes were filmed in the area. As visitors to Kraków discover Kazimierz, new hotels, cafés and restaurants are moving in, and there are signs that young Krakovians now see it as more than the devastating reminder of a tragic period in Polish history.

The easiest way to get to Kazimierz is to walk from the Old Town, but any tram or bus going from the Planty down ul. Stradomska or Starowiślna will have one or two stops in Kazimierz, such as ul. Miodowa or Plac Wolnica. If walking from Wawel Hill, take ul. Stradomska (which becomes ul. Krakowska) south and turn left at ul. Józefa.

There are fewer and fewer dilapidated buildings now but still among the new businesses in the Jewish quarter you can

A cosy Kazimierz café

see many signs of Jewish life in Kazimierz. Eight synagogues (of the 30 that once existed here) survived the war, of which a couple have been established as museums. Ul. Szeroka, which means Wide Street but is actually more of a square, was the heart of the district from the 15th century onwards. On the west side of the square is the **Remu'h Synagogue and Cemetery** (ul. Szeroka 40; 9am–4pm; charge), a small 500-year-old synagogue that is currently being renovated. The second-oldest in the district, it is perhaps the most important synagogue in the area today. Jews visit to touch the chair of the 16th-century Rabbi Moses Isserles, a great philosopher and lawyer, and a black feast calendar is one of the few surviving elements of the original synagogue. Much

Remu'h Cemetery

of the cemetery next door was destroyed by the Nazis, though several hundred gravestones, many of them 400 years old and buried by the Jews to avoid desecration by invaders of the 18th century, were discovered during excavations after the war. The handful of tombs enclosed by a fence includes that of Rabbi Isserles, which is often covered with small stones, measures of respect left behind by Jewish visitors. The Wailing Wall at one end of the cemetery is made up of fragments of gravestones that were destroyed by the Germans.

At the south end of ul. Szeroka is the **Old Synagogue** (ul. Szeroka 24; Apr–Oct Mon 10am–2pm, Tue–Sun 9am–5pm; Nov–Mar Mon 10am–2pm, Tue–Thu, Sat–Sun 9am–4pm, till 5pm on Fri; charge, Mon free). Dating from the 15th century, it is the oldest surviving Jewish house of worship in Poland. Today it houses a museum of Jewish history and culture (www.mhk.pl), with an ornate

Jewish culture

Now running for over 20 years, the annual Jewish Festival of Culture is a great way to discover both Kraków's Jewish past and the vibrant Jewish culture that remains in the city. Highlights of the 10-day festival include kosher cooking, Hassidic dancing and some of the best Klezmer music you'll hear. For more information, see www.jewishfestival.pl.

16th-century wrought-iron bimah, or pulpit, in the centre of the main prayer hall. A monument in front of the museum marks the site where 30 Polish men and boys were executed by Nazis in 1943. A plaque marks the spot where Polish revolutionary Tadeusz Kościuszko rallied the Jews to join his fight for Polish independence in 1794.

One street to the west is the large **Isaac Synagogue** (ul. Kupa 18; Sun–Fri 9am–7pm; charge), a cavernous hall that was once the most beautiful of all the synagogues here, with opulent Baroque stucco decoration from the mid-17th century that was destroyed by the Nazis, though restoration work is under way. Today, at the end of the otherwise empty room, school groups and other visitors sit silently in front of televisions and watch a sombre documentary of Jewish life (The Memory of Polish Jews) set to plaintive music that evokes the Holocaust. Next to the synagogue is an atmospheric, bohemian café, **Singer**, where some of the tables are old Singer sewing machine stands and which can be credited with inspiring many lace-strewn imitators in the area.

The **Jewish Cultural Centre** (ul. Rabina Meiselsa 17; Mon–Fri 10am–6pm, Sat–Sun 10am–2pm; www.judaica.pl) is located just west of pl. Nowy, the old Jewish marketplace. It has regular exhibitions and conferences aimed at preserving knowledge of Jewish culture. A superb photographic exhibition of Jewish heritage can be seen at the **Galicia Jewish Museum** (ul. Dajwór 18; daily 9am–8pm; charge; www.galiciajewishmuseum.org), which also runs a very full programme of cultural events and is a good place to begin to make sense of what you see in Kazimierz.

Western Kazimierz is the Catholic section of the planned town and is marked by three churches: **Corpus Christi Church** (Kościół Bożego Ciała; ul. Bożego Ciała 26), the Gothic **St Catherine's Church** (Kościół Św. Katarzyny; ul. Augustiańska 7) and the **Pauline Church** (Kościół Paulinów; ul. Skałeczna), known as 'the Church on the Rock'. Celebrated cultural figures, including Stanisław Wyspiański and Nobel winner Czesław Miłosz, are buried in the crypt of the latter. On pl. Wolnica is the old town hall, which now houses an **Ethnographic Museum** (Muzeum Etnograficzne; pl. Wolnica 1; Tue–Sun 10am–7pm; http://etnomuzeum.eu).

The **New Jewish Cemetery** (Nowy Cmentarz Żydowski; ul. Miodowa 55; Sun–Fri 9am–5pm), a short walk northeast of ul. Szeroka, is a large, haunted-looking place of toppled gravestones with Yiddish insignias and lettering grown over by bright green moss. The cemetery was founded in 1800 and is the only current burial place for Jews in Kraków.

The actual ghetto where the Nazis forced the Jews to live between 1941 and 1943 is located across the river over

In the ghetto

Jews in the war-time ghetto were required by the Nazis to: have a Star of David designating all businesses; carry Jewish identity cards at all times; and ride on the back half of trams, which were labelled *Für Juden* (for Jews).

Powstańców Śląskich bridge at the end of ul. Starowiślna, in the Podgórze district. The **Under the Eagle Pharmacy** (Apteka pod Orłem; pl. Bohaterów Getta 18; 10am–7pm), which along with Pomorska Street and Oskar Schindler's Enamel Factory constitute the so called 'Memory Trail' (www.mhk.pl/memory-trail). These three branches of the Historical Museum of the City of Kraków tell the story of Kraków over the years 1939–1956. Now a small museum of Jewish life in the ghetto, the pharmacy once belonged to a Pole, Tadeusz Pankiewicz, the only Gentile

Commemorating Jewish history in the Galicia Museum

whom the Germans allowed to live in the ghetto. He later was one of the critical witnesses at the Nuremberg trials. Nearby, off ul. Lwowska is a still-standing section of the wall that the Nazis constructed around the ghetto. Designed to mimic the form of traditional Jewish gravestones, the message delivered a clear 'here is where you shall die'.

Across pl. Bohaterów Ghetta (Heros of the Ghetto Square) Oskar Schindler's former Emalia enamel factory is now home to a 'factory of memory', a powerful multimedia exhibition of the Nazi Occupation of 1939–45 (Fabryka Schindlera; ul. Lipowa 4; Apr–Oct Mon 10am–4pm, Tue–Sun 9am–8pm; Nov–Mar Mon 10am–2pm, Tue–Sun 10am–6pm, Mon free; last admission 90 mins before closing; under-14s must be accompanied;

Photograph in the Museum of National Remembrance

www.bilety.mhk.pl to reserve advance tickets online). Next door, the former factory floor houses the **Museum of Contemporary Art in Krakow** (MOCAK, Muzeum Sztuki Współczesnej w Krakowie; Tue–Sun 11–7pm; Tue free; www.mocak.pl), which hosts temporary exhibitions of international art.

Most visitors to Kraków stick to the Old Town and Wawel Hill, and perhaps Kazimierz and separate trips to Auschwitz and the Wieliczka Salt Mines. If you have more time, though, just west of the Old Town is the main building of the **National Museum** (Muzeum Narodowe; al. 3 Maja 1; Tue–Sat 10am–6pm, Sun 10am–4pm, Mon closed; Sun permanent collection free; www.muzeum.krakow.pl). The off-putting, Soviet-style architecture houses an important collection including 14th-century stained glass and decorative arts, furniture and vestments from Wawel, a wonderful collection of paintings, sculptures and other works by leading 20th-century Polish artists and a wide array of military armaments and uniforms, of great interest to history enthusiasts. It also hosts most of the important touring exhibitions that come to Kraków.

Those interested in architecture and Oriental culture should visit **Manggha** (ul. Konopnickiej 26; Tue–Sun 10am–6pm, free on Tue; http://manggha.pl), across the river south of Wawel Hill and west of Kazimierz. The futuristic building was designed by the Japanese architect Arata Isozaki and funded by celebrated Polish film director Andrzej Wajda. It operates as a cultural centre hosting temporary exhibitions-mainly of Oriental Art and it has a pleasant café that serves good sushi.

EXCURSIONS FROM KRAKOW

WIELICZKA SALT MINES

Wieliczka ❷ (ul. Daniłowicza 10, Wieliczka; daily for guided tours only; Apr–Oct 7.30am–7.30pm; Nov–Mar 8am–5pm; www.kopalnia.pl), a series of deep mines more than 700 years old located about 10km (6 miles) southeast of Kraków, makes for an extraordinary subterranean adventure. The mine reaches 327m (1,073ft) and nine levels underground. Visitors descend 378 steps down to the first level of 64m (210ft) and then pass through 2km (1.25 miles) of tunnels, visiting some 20 chambers and chapels carved out of salt by miners. The Baroque St Anthony Chapel dates to 1690–1710, but the largest and

OSKAR SCHINDLER

Immortalised first in Thomas Keneally's book *Schindler's Ark* and later in the Oscar-winning film *Schindler's List*, directed by Steven Spielberg, the enigmatic German businessman Oskar Schindler (1908–74) lived and worked in Kraków during World War II. He bought a bankrupt enamel factory in Podgórze and employed cheap Jewish labour, saving thousands of lives by bribing and hoodwinking scores of high-ranking Nazis throughout the war. His famous list dates from the summer of 1944, and was made up of 1,100 Jewish men, women and children destined for the gas chambers at Auschwitz whom he saved by sending to another factory he owned in what is now the Czech Republic. After his death Schindler was buried on Jerusalem's Mount Zion, recognised as one of the Righteous Among Nations.

Inside Wieliczka Salt Mine

most astounding chapel is the **Chapel of the Blessed St Kinga**. Like the other chambers, everything in it is carved out of salt. Its chandeliers, altar and remarkable relief carving (with great perspective) of the Last Supper were created over a period of 70 years, and were begun, in the 19th century, by just three miners, who were obviously talented and dedicated sculptors (like all the chapels and chambers, this massive hall was carved in the miners' time off). Weddings are occasionally held in the St Kinga Chapel, as is Mass three times a year. Along the way in other chambers you'll also see green-salt statues of Copernicus and, rather curiously, the Seven Dwarves.

Listed by Unesco as a World Heritage Site, the mine was the property of the Polish Royal Family (for whom the salt, called 'grey gold', contributed one-third of the total royal wealth) until the 1772 partition of Poland, when it fell to the Austrians. Salt mining continued here until 1996, and today the mine is visited by tour groups and those seeking relief from respiratory ailments like asthma in the sanatorium 135m (450ft) below ground. During World War II, the Nazis used the tallest chamber (which measures 36m/118ft from floor to ceiling) as a secret factory for the manufacture of aircraft parts, staffed by Jewish prisoners. A few years back, a couple of thrillseekers pulled off a bungee jump and others conducted the first underground balloon flight, documented by the Guinness Book of World Records, in the same chamber. During July and August, a miners' orchestra plays in the lake chamber, treating visitors to a 170-year-old tradition, and the mine is a popular venue for jazz concerts and other special events.

At the end of the three-hour visit to the mine, you can visit the museum of mining equipment and geological specimens or stop for a bite at the underground snack bar before being whisked back to ground level by a wooden elevator.

Admission to the Wieliczka mines is by guided tour only. Individuals can join tour groups with commentaries in various languages including English and Polish (advance booking is recommended to avoid waiting to join a tour in the language of your choice). To get to Wieliczka, the cheapest and most efficient means is to take a contrabus marked Wieliczka–Kraków from the train station in Kraków.

AUSCHWITZ AND BIRKENAU

Poland was ground zero for Nazi Germany's terrible campaign to rid the world of all Jews, and the Auschwitz concentration camp was one of the most efficient elements in their killing machine. Visiting it and neighbouring Birkenau is a chilling and unforgettable experience. Tour slots can be reserved online in advance at visit.auschwitz.org. Both Auschwitz (or Auschwitz I to give it its proper name) and Birkenau (Auschwitz II) are in the town of Oświęcim (Auschwitz being the Germanised version of the name), 75km (47 miles) west of Kraków.

At Birkenau, an inscription bluntly reads: 'Forever let this place be a cry of despair and a warning to Humanity, where the Nazis murdered about one and a half million men,

Getting there

To get to Auschwitz, you can take a 2-hour train or frequent bus (90 minutes; Nos 2–5 or 24–30) leaving from in front of Kraków's train station. However, you will need to take a taxi or walk to Birkenau from Auschwitz, as there is no frequent bus service. Alternatively, you could sign up for one of the many package tours offered by any travel agency in Kraków.

women, and children, mainly Jews from various countries of Europe.' The horrors of the acts that were carried out here, and the reality of lost lives and potential, are unfathomable.

Auschwitz ❸ (daily Feb 8am–4pm; Mar, Oct 8am–5pm; Apr, May, Sept 8am–6pm; June–Aug 8am–7pm; Nov, Jan 8am–3pm; Dec 8am–2pm; free; www.ausch witz.org) was originally a Polish army barracks. Jews from as far away as Norway and Greece were loaded into wretched, sealed trains with no water, food or lavatories, and very little air to breathe, and herded to the concentration camps in Poland. The first 728 'prisoners of war', most of them Polish and all of them from the town of Tarnów, were brought here in June 1940. After that, streams of Jews, as well as Soviet prisoners, were relocated to the camps. They became slave labourers; many died of starvation, while some were summarily executed and many others were herded into gas chambers and killed with lethal Zyklon B gas.

A short and disturbing documentary film is shown in English, German and French at regular intervals. It features original footage, shot by the Soviet troops who liberated the camp in 1945, and is a good, if startling, introduction to trying to comprehend what you're about to see when you go in. After viewing the film, pass under the formiddable entrance gates to Auschwitz, which are inscribed with the cruel slogan *Arbeit Macht Frei* (Work Makes Free).

About 30 cell blocks, as well as watchtowers and barbed-wire fences, survived the Nazi attempt to destroy the camp when they fled at the conclusion of the war. You can walk freely among the blocks and enter those that are open. In one, behind glass cases you'll see collections of piles of shoes, twisted spectacles, tons of human hair, and suitcases with the names and addresses of prisoners – who were told they were simply being relocated to a new town – stencilled on them. Hallways are lined with rows of mug shots of the prisoners, some adorned with flowers from surviving family members. Outside Block 11, the so-called 'Block of Death', is an execution wall where prisoners were shot. Inside is where the Nazis carried out their first experiments gassing prisoners with Zyklon B. Another barrack nearby is dedicated to the 'Martyrdom of the Jewish People'. At the end of the exhibit of historical documents and photographs, a haunting and mournful soundtrack,

Lookout tower and barbed wire, Auschwitz

Birkenau

the song Oh God the Merciful, plays while the names of the people killed at death camps are read.

Birkenau (same hours as Auschwitz I, visitors may take a bus or walk between the two; free), about 3km (2 miles) from Auschwitz, was built in 1941 when Hitler went beyond simply collecting political prisoners and embarked on a mass extermination programme. Its 300 long barracks on 175 hectares (523 acres) served as holding cells for the most murderous machinery of Hitler's extermination 'solution' for the Jews. Approximately three-quarters of all the Jews deported to Birkenau were gassed upon arrival. Indeed, Birkenau was the very definition of a death camp: it had its own railway station for transporting prisoners, four huge gas chambers, each of which was capable of gassing 2,000 prisoners at a time, and crematoria were outfitted with electric lifts to take the bodies to the ovens.

Visitors can climb to the second storey of the principal watchtower at the entrance, from where it is apparent just how vast this camp was. Stretching out are seemingly unending lines of barracks, watchtowers and barbed-wire fences; the camp could hold a total of 200,000 inmates. At the rear of the camp, beyond a grisly pond where the ashes of the murdered were dumped, is an enigmatic monument to the dead of the Holocaust, with inscriptions in the 20 languages of the prisoners who were murdered at Auschwitz and Birkenau.

ZAKOPANE AND THE TATRA MOUNTAINS

Europe's second-largest chain of mountains after the Alps, the Carpathian Mountains (Karpaty), extending along the southern border of Poland, are where many Poles go to relax. It is a beautiful area of forests, lakes, historic mountain towns and spa villages, with great hiking and skiing opportunities. The High Tatras are the highest range of the Carpathians. Established tourist facilities make many areas within these mountain chains readily accessible. The most attractive town in the area is Zakopane, almost on the border with Slovakia. Zakopane is also Poland's unofficial winter capital. A two-hour drive south of Kraków, it is easily reached by buses that leave frequently from Kraków's main PKS bus station; and though road traffic can be bad in peak seasons, trains are considerably slower with journey times of over four hours.

Spectacular views near Zakopane

ZAKOPANE

A small, Alpine-like village, **Zakopane ④** is undeniably appealing, with a terrific backdrop of snow-capped mountains and wooden chalets built in the distinctive local, so-called Zakopane Style. A remote mountain outpost until it began to gain notice in the late 1800s, Zakopane is popular for both winter and summer holidays, drawing more than two million visitors a year, who come here for outdoor sports and shopping. It is also a centre of Górale (mountain people) folk art, traditional mountain music, and a unique style of wooden highlander architecture that was elevated to high art in the mid-19th century by several notable artists and architects.

Zakopane chalets

The village's main drag is the pedestrian-only shopping street ul. Krupówki. There are several interesting wooden buildings, horse carriages for hire, and sellers of folk art and local snacks. At the lower end of the promenade, the **Tatra Museum** (Muzeum Tatrzańskie; ul. Krupówki 10; Wed–Sat 9am–5pm, also Sun 9am–3pm; www.muzeumtatrzanskie.com.pl) houses a collection of local folk art and exhibits on local flora and fauna.

At the end of ul. Krupówki, turn left at ul. Kościeliska. About 200m (650ft) along on the right side is the old parish **St Mary of Częstochowa**

Church (Kościół Matki Bos-kiej Częstochowskiej; ul. Kościeliska 4; daily 9.30am–4pm), a splendid, tiny rustic wooden chapel dating from 1847. Next to it is an old cemetery, **Stary Cmentarz**, populated with a fascinating array of carved wooden tombstones and gravemarkers, demonstrating the highly creative mountain artistry.

Skiing in the Tatra Mountains

The wooden homes nearby are excellent examples of the Zakopane Style, which features highly decorative carved wood.

Zakopane has earned a reputation as an artists' village, and there are several galleries and small museums of interest. One is the **Władysław Hasior Gallery** (Galeria Władysława Hasiora; ul. Jagiellońska 18b; Wed–Sat 11am–6pm, Sun 9am–3pm). This branch of the Tatra Museum, close to the train station shows the works of the artist Władysław Hasior (1928–99), who was closely associated with Zakopane.

THE TATRAS

At the foot of the **Tatras**, Zakopane is blessed with one of the most spectacular landscapes in Poland. Even if you haven't come to ski, it's fun and worthwhile to take the cable car up to **Mt Kasprowy** for the splendid views of the mountains, hiking trails and ski slopes above the town. The ride in a modern cable car takes about 12 minutes long with a stop at an intermediate station. It takes you (and crowds of skiers in winter) up to the summit of Mt Kasprowy Wierch, at 1,959m (6427ft). There you can stand with one foot in Poland, the other in Slovakia. Reasonably priced return cable car tickets give you a mandatory 100 minutes at the top, so if you don't have skis or don't plan to hike, you might want to bring a book. In summer, many people take the ride up and walk back down along a series of marked trails (about 2 hours). To get to the cable car station in Kuźnice (south of Zakopane), take a taxi, bus No. 7 from directly in front of the bus station, or a minibus across the street from the bus stop.

If you're interested in hiking excursions in the area, including everything from easy walks through valleys to hardcore Tatra excursions to beautiful lakes, enquire at the rustic-looking **tourism office** (ul. Kościuszki 17; Mon–Sat 9am–5pm,), near the bus station. The Tatras are for serious mountaineers only, and require special equipment and a guide. Less taxing nature spots suitable for day-long hiking include the valleys Dolina Białego, Dolina Strążyska, Dolina Chochołowska and Dolina Kościeliska.

The International Festival of Highland Culture is held every August in Zakopane. Essentially a week-long mountain

WITKACY

Warsaw-born Stanisław Ignacy Witkiewicz (1885–1939), aka Witkacy, was a gifted and eccentric painter, photographer and playwright whose strange life is part of Zakopane legend. Accused of murdering his fiancée in 1914, Witkacy set off on a voyage of discovery that took him to Australia, from where he returned to fight the Germans, create some puzzling, drug-induced work, descend into bouts of depression and start a theatre company in Zakopane that still bears his name. Witkacy took his own life when the Red Army invaded Poland in 1939 and was buried first in a remote part of Ukraine before being returned to Zakopane in 1988. In one final Witkacy-style twist, the wrong body was returned and his corpse has been lost for all eternity.

folklore contest and full schedule of concerts, music competitions and parades, it has been held since 1965, and is an excellent introduction to the unique mountain culture of the Górale people.

MAŁOPOLSKA

Małopolska, or Little Poland, was once the name of the whole southeast corner of the country between Kraków and Ukraine, but is now broken up into small provinces or voivodships. The small and agreeably sleepy town of **Sandomierz** ❺ is a handsome former trading port on

Town Hall, Old Town, Sandomierz

the banks of the Vistula. One of Poland's most ancient towns, it prospered during the Renaissance. Its old town, on a hill above the river, has a smattering of fine buildings, including the town hall on the Rynek, or market square, a 14th-century cathedral and castle, and St James's Church, founded in 1226 and one of the oldest brick churches in Poland. Of particular interest to visitors is the underground route that dips into a couple of dozen cellars beneath the townhouses on the Rynek.

ZAMOŚĆ

The small Renaissance town of **Zamość** ❻ (Lubelski voivodship) is one of Poland's little gems. The Old Town has more than 100 buildings and monuments of artistic and historic distinction. The city was planned by the politician and nobleman

Jan Zamoyski (1542–1605), who sought to build a perfect city, enclosed within fortifications, in the centre of the Lublin Upland. To carry out his plan, Zamoyski commissioned an Italian architect from Padua, Bernardo Morando, in 1580. The town's strategic location on important East–West trade routes resulted in considerable prosperity in the 17th century. Its fortifications were so strong that it was impregnable to the Tartars and Cossacks in the early 17th century, and was one of only three cities in Poland able to resist the Swedish Deluge of 1656.

Zamość's **Market Square** (Rynek), dominated by a large, pink town hall with a tall Baroque clock tower, is one of Poland's most splendid. To the right of the town hall are richly ornamented and arcaded houses painted vivid green, yellow, brick-red and blue, with Oriental detailing of 17th-century Armenian merchants. The other houses on the remaining three sides of the square are plainer and painted in more

The pretty Market Square, Zamość

subtle pastels, but don't detract from the square's great harmony. On each side of the Rynek are eight houses (save the north side, which is dominated by the town hall).

On the north side of the Rynek is the **Zamojskie Museum** (Muzeum Zamojskie; ul. Ormiańska 30; Tue–Sun, Oct–Apr 9am–4pm; May–Sept 9am–5pm; http://muzeum-zamojskie.pl), which houses an array of items ranging from archaeological finds to armaments and religious sculptures, including an interesting clay model of the Zamość Old Town and paintings of the Zamoyski clan. More importantly, the museum is an opportunity to walk through the interior of two of the grand old burgher houses on the Rynek. Much of the houses' rich detailing – stone carving, frescoes around the top of rooms, and handsome wood-beam ceilings – have been well restored. The most recent addition is the Arsenal Museum of Fortifications and Weaponry (ul. Zamkowa 2; http://muzeumarsenal.pl). Just north of the Rynek is the former Jewish Quarter. In its heyday, Zamość was a multicultural city; Jews, Armenians, Germans, Greeks, Turks, Dutch and Italians all came to the city to trade. The former synagogue here has been restored and was recently opened as a modern cultural centre.

West of the Rynek is the large but rather plain **Lord's Resurrection and St Thomas the Apostle Cathedral** (Katedra pw. Zmartwychwstania Pańskiego i Św. Tomasza Apostoła; ul. Kolegiacka 2). To its immediate south, the **Religious Museum** (Muzeum Sakralne Katedry Zamojskiej; ul. Kolegiacka 1a; weekdays 10am–6pm; Sat–Sun 1–6pm; www.katedra.zamojskolubaczowska.pl) is a small, three-room collection of mostly Renaissance religious objects and paintings with curious translations into English.

On the eastern edge of the Old Town is the one surviving bastion of the seven that once formed the massive fortifications surrounding Zamość. The **Lvov Gate** (Brama Lwowska),

The view from Three Crosses Hill, Kazimierz Dolny

next to a large and rather uninteresting market, is one of three original entrances to the city. Across from it is the large **Franciscan Church** (Kościół Franciszkanów), which retains none of its Baroque splendour, as it was destroyed when occupiers transformed it into a hospital and then military barracks.

Even though Zamość is a Unesco World Heritage Site, its citizens still appear to be unaccustomed to the curious attentions and cameras of tourists in their midst. This makes it a good place to see a very pretty and exceedingly well-preserved little town where the citizens don't all speak English, and go about their business with little regard for the złoty of outsiders. On the other hand, if you're looking for something to do after taking in the main square and handful of streets that define Zamość's relaxed Old Town, you might be better off moving on to Kraków or Warsaw. If that's the case, there are regular bus and train services that take about 5–6 hours to either destination, though the connections from Lublin are faster and more frequent.

KAZIMIERZ DOLNY

Also in the Lubelski voivodship, the small, charming mercantile town **Kazimierz Dolny ❼**, perched on the banks of the Vistula, became wealthy from the grain trade in the 16th century. Kazimierz has become a popular day-trip from Warsaw, and is likely to be busy on summer weekends.

The Old Town is notable for several fine burgher's town houses with elaborate Renaissance stucco work around the Rynek, or Market Square, which is also distinguished by a central wooden well. A couple of small museums – the Goldsmith Museum and the fine Celejowska House (both are branches of the Muzeum Nadwiślańskie; www.mnkd.pl) telling the story of the town – are also worth exploring.

The ruins of the town's 14th-century castle, a short walk northeast of the Rynek, provide good views above the river, though they're better at the watchtower a little further up the hill and best at Three Crosses Hilltop, a steep climb east of the Rynek. You can reach it returning from the watchtower.

WARSAW

King Sigismund Vasa moved the royal court from the ancient city of Kraków to **Warsaw ❽**, on the banks of the River Vistula (Wisła) in the centre of the country, in 1596. Though Kraków would remain the cultural and spiritual heart of Poland, the new political and administrative centre in Warsaw grew rapidly, adding wide boulevards and palatial residences to the small Old and New Towns.

Over the centuries, the city suffered from repeated invasions, occupations and destruction and had to be rebuilt on several occasions. World War II proved to be far more devastating and tragic than any of the previous conflicts; towards the end of the war, after the Warsaw Uprising and with the Soviet Red Army advancing inexorably, Hitler gave orders

Libeskind's skyscraper, Warsaw

for the entire city to be systematically destroyed, and Warsaw was almost entirely levelled. Miraculously, the Old Town was later studiously rebuilt, according to old photographs, paintings and architectural plans.

Though Warsaw is the nation's capital, it usually proves less captivating to visitors than Kraków or Gdańsk. In part, this is because it is still a city in transition, leading the way for the new post-Communist Poland – Poland as a member of NATO and the European Union. Outside the Old Town, the city can be unattractive – the architecture a haphazard and sometimes ugly mix of Stalinist concrete tower blocks, older buildings in need of restoration, and gleaming modern towers, all constructed with little thought given to urban planning. Neighbourhoods are somewhat difficult to define. Still, it's a dynamic city of more than 1.7 million people with an important Royal Way, stunningly rejuvenated historic centre, reminders of the Warsaw Ghetto and monuments of Jewish legacy, and an important cultural nucleus.

The Vistula divides Warsaw down the middle, but almost everything of interest to visitors is located on the west bank. The Royal Way, the focus of most sightseeing, stretches from the Old Town south to Łazienki Park and Wilanów, formerly a royal summer palace.

THE OLD TOWN AND MARKET SQUARE

Warsaw's **Old Town** (Stare Miasto) would be remarkable even if it hadn't been rebuilt from scratch after being razed during World War II. How extensive was the annihilation? Some historians estimate that 85 percent of the Old Town was destroyed. It is impossible not to marvel that within a period of around 30 years from the war's end, the entire Old Town was resurrected with abundant care for the architecture, aesthetics and soul of Warsaw. Competition for rebuilding projects was intense, and in fact, many other towns were neglected because of the resources directed to Warsaw. Incredibly, it looks, and more importantly feels, authentic, like a town with a medieval layout and Renaissance façades. The reconstructed town is a true testament to a people who refused to be defeated, even though the city's population had been reduced by more than two-thirds. Although some of the buildings only date from the mid-1950s, the Old Town was added in its entirety to Unesco's list of World Heritage Sites in 1980.

THE ROYAL CASTLE

It's probably best to begin a tour of Warsaw at the entrance to the Old Town, **Plac Zamkowy** Ⓐ (Castle Square). A tall column with a bronze **statue of King Sigismund** – who moved the capital to Warsaw – marks the square, against a backdrop of vibrantly coloured pastel town houses with red tile roofs. The fortifications that once enclosed the Old Town were dismantled in the 19th century, though you can still see fragments of them on one side of the square.

On the eastern side of the square is the massive **Royal Castle** Ⓑ (Zamek Królewski; pl. Zamkowy 4; Oct–Apr Tue–Sat 10am–4pm, Sun 11am–4pm; May–Sept Mon–Sat 10am–6pm, till 8pm on Thu, Sun 11am–6pm; www.zamek-krolewski.pl). Although a fortress was first established on this spot in the 1300s, the

Warsaw Rising

This museum (Muzeum Powstania Warszawskiego, ul. Grzybowska 79, tel: 022 539 7905; Mon, Wed, Fri 8am–6pm, Thur 8am–8pm, Sat–Sun 10am–6pm; www.1944.pl) tells the story of the doomed Warsaw Uprising and hence of Poland's fate in World War II, with audiovisual displays as well as thousands of objects.

present structure is, like the whole of its surroundings, a recent 20th-century reconstruction. In 1944, it was little more than a smoking pile of rubble, with all its great interiors destroyed by bullets, dynamite and fire. Almost all the royal collection of great works of art and tapestries was stolen or destroyed, though it should be noted that many pieces, including furnishings, were removed for safekeeping when the war broke out. Reconstruction did not begin until 1971, and the Castle was reopened to the public in 1984.

As visitors to the castle pass through the stately rooms with excellent stucco detailing and lush works of art (some of which are copies of originals), they have to keep reminding themselves that what they are seeing was is actually little more than 30 years' old. Fragments of original building materials, including decorative carvings and elements of stucco, were used in every possible case, and, if you look hard enough, you may be able to distinguish the old from the new.

The Royal Castle was the official residence of the kings of Poland from the 17th century onwards, and it is where Poland's landmark Constitution – the second oldest in the world, after that of the United States – was passed by the Sejm (parliament) on 3 May 1791. There are separate charges for visiting different parts of the castle. If time is limited it is probably best to visit the main parts of the interior on the ticket that gives entry to the upper-level Great and King's apartments (including the Great Assembly Room, the National

Hall, the Throne Room, the Bedroom, the Old Audience Hall, the Canaletto Room, the Chapel and the Marble Room), so you will see the true highlights of the Castle.

The **King Stanisław August apartments** are among the most opulent rooms in the castle. On the upper level, the massive, mid-18th-century Ballroom – used variously as a concert hall, meeting and audience room, and the first room to be destroyed in 1939 – is perhaps the most stunning of all the rooms. Note the aptly named ceiling painting (a reconstruction), *The Dissolution of Chaos*.

The **Canaletto Room** showcases detailed paintings of Warsaw's Old Town architecture, by his pupil the Italian Bernardo Bellotto; these paintings survived the war and were instrumental in the capital's reconstruction efforts. In the **Marble Room**, another highlight, you'll see portraits of the 22 kings of Poland. The **Throne Room** glitters with a red-and-gold

Royal Castle and Zygmund Column in the Old Town

Evening performers in the Old Town

canopy of handmade silver-embroidered eagles. The originals were stolen by the Germans, but one eagle was recovered in the United States in 1991. It was bought by the Castle, and from it the entire canopy was reconstructed.

If you have more time, separate tickets will give you entry to the **Tin-Roofed Palace**, which was the apartment of Prince Joseph Poniatowski, where there is an exhibition of Oriental carpets; the Lanckoroński art collection, which includes paintings by Rembrandt; the coin exhibition and certain temporary exhibitions, though entry to the historic Kubicki Arcades and the displays about the castle's reconstruction are free.

ST JOHN'S CATHEDRAL

From Plac Zamkowy, head north along ul. Świętojańska. On the right is **St John's Cathedral ©** (Archikatedra Św. Jana), the oldest in Warsaw, dating from the 14th century. The cathedral was largely levelled during the war; though the Gothic brick exterior was rebuilt, too much of the interior was lost, and the Cathedral now looks wholly different from when the last king of Poland, Stanisław August Poniatowski, was crowned and buried here in 1764. The crypt holds the tombs of several famous Poles, among them the dukes of Mazovia, the Nobel Prize-winning writer Henryk Sienkiewicz, and the first president of Poland, Gabriel Narutowicz. St John's played a role during the 1944 Warsaw Uprising against the German occupiers. German tanks even entered the confines of the church. If you walk around the outside to the south wall, you'll see lodged in the stone actual fragments of the heavy equipment used by the Nazis to tear down the Old Town.

AROUND THE RYNEK

Head a little further north to the heart of the Old Town, the lively **Old Town Market Square** (Rynek Starego Miasta). The compact square is one of Poland's finest, an unusually harmonious colourful ensemble of mostly four-storey 16th- to 18th-century (style) merchants' houses, each with wonderful individual Gothic, Baroque and Renaissance architectural features. It's simply an amazing story of reconstruction; it's hard to believe the square is a replica of what stood here before the war. In the centre of the Rynek are two water pumps and a statue of Syrena, the Warsaw mermaid of ancient legend. The square is popular with visitors, who frequent the many excellent, if relatively expensive, restaurants in the ground floors and cellars of several of the town houses. The area is particularly lively in summer, when it's covered with café tables, there are artists and buskers aplenty, and horse-drawn carriages trundle to and fro for the delight of tourists. Keep an eye out for the excellent, free open air jazz concerts on Saturdays in summer.

On the northern side of the Rynek extends the **Warsaw Museum** (Muzeum Warszawy; Rynek Starego Miasta 28–42; http://muzeumwarszawy.pl), currently under renovation. The museum has several branches across the city (see website), but the main building won't re-open until mid-2017.

Beyond the Market Square, the cobblestone streets lead to attractive little corners, quiet courtyards and narrow passageways. It's a great place to wander, day or night, though you should of course exercise caution after dark. Don't miss the area behind the cathedral, where you'll find a small, pretty square (Kanonia) and a terrace with views across the Vistula. Northwest of the Rynek, on ul. Podwale, is the **Monument to the Little Insurgent** (Pomnik Małego Powstańca), a bronze statue of a small boy half hidden under a giant military helmet and carrying an automatic rifle, a symbol of the young children who fought alongside adults in the 1944 Warsaw Uprising against the Nazis. North of the Market Square, ul. Nowomiejska leads to defensive walls, largely rebuilt, and the semicircular Gothic **Barbican** (Barbakan), standing over a moat at what was the northern gate to the city. The area is a popular haunt of street artists and entertainers. A small exposition inside the Barbican can be visited in summer (Tue–Sun 10am–7pm).

Beyond the Barbican is the **New Town** (Nowe Miasto), into which Warsaw expanded after outgrowing the walled Old Town in the 15th century. The two parts were not officially linked until the 18th century. Since it was created as a separate town, the New Town not only has a similar layout to the Old Town, it has its own parish church and town hall. There are several churches in the New Town, including the diminutive Baroque **Church of the Nuns of the Holy Sacrament** (Kościół Sakramentek) dedicated to St Kazimierz on the **New Town Market Square** ⓓ (Rynek Nowego Miasta).

Look also for the **Maria Skłodowska-Curie Museum** ⓔ (Muzeum Marii Skłodowskiej-Curie; ul. Freta 5; June–Aug Tue–Sun 10am–7pm; Sep–May Tue–Sun 9am–4.30; http://muzeum-msc.pl), just down the street from the Barbican. Maria Skłodowska

(1867–1934), or Marie Curie as she's better known, was born in Warsaw, though she lived most of her adult life in France. A scientist and physician, she was the first woman to teach at the Sorbonne in Paris. She discovered radium and polonium and the phenomenon of radioactivity. She was the first woman to win the Nobel Prize in 1903 (for physics) and in 1911 (for chemistry).

When you need a break from sightseeing, keep in mind that the New Town is also known for its restaurants and cafés.

Syrena, the mermaid of Warsaw, in the city's Market Square

THE ROYAL WAY

The **Royal Way** is the elegant 4-km (2.5-mile) route along which the Polish monarchy travelled south from their official residence, the Royal Castle, to the summer palace, Łazienki. The route is lined with palaces, churches, town houses, museums and monuments along or just off the main streets of ul. Krakowskie Przedmieście, ul. Nowy Świat and al. Ujazdowskie.

Ul. Krakowskie Przedmieście, the first stretch of the route, is one of Warsaw's classic streets. **St Anne's Church** (Kościół Św. Anny; ul. Krakowskie Przedmieście 68) was built in the 15th century and reconstructed in the Baroque style after it was plundered by Swedish troops. One of the few major churches to avoid devastation in World War II, its observation tower has great views of the Royal Castle and Old Town. To take a detour, walk a couple of blocks west along ul. Senatorska to pl. Teatralny, which is dominated by the **Teatr Wielki – Opera Narodowa ❼** (Great Theatre – National Opera; pl. Teatralny 1; http://teatrwielki.pl), Poland's greatest opera and ballet institution, built in 1833. It was bombed during World War II, with only its façade surviving the blasts. It was rebuilt and reconfigured inside and now has the largest stage in the world.

Back on ul. Krakowskie Przedmieście, as you head south, you'll pass a **statue of Adam Mickiewicz**, Poland's revered Romantic poet. Further south is the white neo-Classical **Presidential Palace ❼**, the residence of the president of Poland. At the front are four stone lions and a statue of Prince Józef Poniatowski, the 19th-century commander-in-chief of the Polish army during Napoleon's Duchy of Warsaw. Across the street is the **Potocki Palace**, now part of Warsaw University. Past the grand Bristol Hotel, built at the turn of the 20th century, is the 18th-century Baroque Church of St. Joseph of the Visitationists (Kościół Wizytek w Warszawie), with a monument to Cardinal Stefan Wyszyński (1901–81), the Primate of Poland from 1948.

The Gothic Barbican

West of the Royal Way, in the midst of Ogród Saski gardens, is the **Tomb of the Unknown Soldier** ⓗ (Grób Nieznanego Żołnierza). Housed within the surviving fragments of the 17th-century Saxon Palace, it was placed here in 1925 as the only section of the palace to survive Nazi bombing. The nearby Metropolitan office building was designed by noted British architect Sir Norman Foster.

Tram tours

Using one of the tram routes in Warsaw (there are around 30 of them in total) is an excellent way to get around. Tram stops and routes are marked in red on most city maps.

South of Potocki Palace, **Warsaw University** ⓘ (Uniwersytet Warszawski) is denoted by massive, handsome gates atop which perches the traditional Polish eagle. It is the capital's top institution of higher learning, in perpetual rivalry with Kraków's Jagiellonian University. Several of the buildings are former palaces; the oldest dates from 1634. The **Church of the Holy Cross** (Kościół Św. Krzyża; ul. Krakowskie Przedmieście 3), across the street from the university, is a mausoleum of sorts for famous Poles, among them the composer Frédéric Chopin. In fact, in accordance with his will, only his heart is here, in an urn; the rest of his remains lie in France.

The statue at a fork in the road is one of Poland's other most famous sons, the great astronomer **Nicolaus Copernicus** (Mikołaj Kopernik). With his theory of a heliocentric universe, Copernicus, as Poles commonly say, 'stopped the sun and moved the earth'. Just beyond this, the boulevard becomes **ul. Nowy Świat**, one of Warsaw's most fashionable, and is lined with chic boutiques and cafés.

Set back from ul. Nowy Świat is Ostrogski Palace, site of the **Frédéric Chopin Museum** ⓙ (Muzeum Fryderyka Chopina; ul. Okólnik 1; Tue–Sun 11am–8pm; Sun free; www. chopin.museum). This lovely palace is full of artefacts and memorabilia from the life of this outstanding classical composer. Nearby are several other palaces, of which the Zamoyski Palace (on ul. Foksal) is one of the most beautiful.

The **National Museum** Ⓚ (Muzeum Narodowe; al. Jerozolimskie 3; Tue–Sun 10am–6pm, till 9pm on Thu; www.mnw.art.pl) holds a huge collection of art – from Roman and Egyptian archaeology and medieval art to antique furniture and large galleries of Polish and European painting totalling some million objects. Don't miss the excellent Faras Gallery – the only permanent exhibition in Europe of Medieval Nubian paintings from the Nile River Valley south of the First Cataract. Continuing south past the controversial fake palm tree on Rondo de Gaulle and past pl. Trzech Krzyży, (Three Crosses Square, the third golden cross is in the hand of the statue of St John Nepomucen), Al. Ujazdowskie is lined with embassies housed in elegant palaces, and nearby

Metropolitan Office Building, Warsaw

are the Sejm (Polish Parliament) and two attractive parks, Ujazdowski and Łazienkowski, the latter especially esteemed by Varsovians.

JEWISH WARSAW

Thousands of Jews arrived in Warsaw in the second half of the 14th century, though they were expelled by royal decree not long after. They were finally allowed to settle in the city again in 1768, and by the start of World War II, approximately 350,000, or 30 percent, of Warsaw's citizens were Jews. It was at that time the largest Jewish community in pre-war Europe. The residential Jewish Quarter, around the Mirów and Muranów districts (between the Palace of Culture and Science and the Jewish Cemetery in the northwest corner of the city), was transformed into a ghetto by the Nazis. After the Warsaw Ghetto Uprising in 1943, German troops moved in and liquidated the ghetto.

Today only about 2,000 Jews live in Warsaw. The most obvious reminders of the former Jewish presence are the dilapidated buildings on **ul. Próżna**, their walls marked with bullet holes and other poignant reminders of devastation. A Jewish foundation has been entrusted with the restoration of these buildings, and work is set to begin. The **Nożyk Synagogue** (Synagoga Nożyków; ul. Twarda 6; http://warszawa.jewish.org.pl), still in use, is the only surviving Jewish house of prayer in the city. Another haunting symbol of Jewish martyrdom is the fragment of the **Ghetto Wall** (ul. Sienna 55), constructed in 1940.

Farther north, the **Jewish Cemetery** (Cmentarz Żydowski), which abuts the Powązkowski Cemetery and was founded in 1806, gives the overpowering impression of neglect: many of the 200,000 gravestones have toppled over and branches have grown over them. A monument on ul. Stawki marks the spot

Tombstone in the Jewish Cemetery, Warsaw

where 300,000 Jews were transported by train from the ghetto to the Treblinka concentration camp.

On ul. Zamenhofa, the **Monument to the Heroes of the Ghetto** (Pomnik Bohaterów Getta) is a tribute to the poorly armed but valiant Jews who rose up against their Nazi oppressors in 1943. The monument, in the spot where the month-long fighting was heaviest, is a bas-relief that incorporates stone that had been ordered by the Third Reich to commemorate its planned victory. Opposite the monument is the **Museum of the History of Polish Jews** ❶ (Muzeum Historii Żydów Polskich Polin; Mon, Tue, Fri 10am–6pm; Wed, Sat, Sun 10am–8pm; www.polin.pl), designed by Finnish architect Rainer Mahlamäki. The core exposition, developed by more than 120 international scholars and displayed in eight galleries, is a fascinating journey through 1,000 years of history. The heritage and culture of Polish Jews is presented through paintings, interactive installations, artefacts, hands-on exhibits and video projections.

WEST OF THE OLD TOWN
The **Powązkowski Cemetery** (Cmentarz Powązkowski; ul. Powązkowska 14) is one of Warsaw's oldest, largest and most spectacular necropolis, with a host of Warsaw's and Poland's most distinguished citizens, from presidents to poets, in their final resting places. The cemetery is full of gravestones and

mausoleums of all shapes and sizes, many obvious testaments to the wealth and prestige of those they shelter. Some are grand, some restrained, some crowned by beautifully expressive sculpture, but all are covered by a dense, light green moss.

Warsaw's **New City Centre**, near the central train station (Warszawa Centralna), roughly equidistant between the Old Town and Łazienki Park, is a busy commercial area, teeming with banks, hotels and shops, and thick with traffic. It's perhaps most notable for the presence of a building that has become a symbol of the city, despite being abhorred by almost all Varsovians. The **Palace of Culture and Science**  (Pałac Kultury i Nauki; pl. Defilad 1; www.pkin.pl), a 1955 Stalinist edifice that was ostensibly a gift of the Russian government to the Polish people, is Warsaw's tallest building, at 231m (758ft) (soon to be superseded by a new 310m tall skyscraper designed by Sir Norman Foster). Inside are many shops and galleries, and an observation deck on the 30th floor affords views of the entire city and surrounding Mazovian plains – when not obscured by smog. Since the collapse of Communism, there has been much debate about what to do with this unpopular building.

Monument to the Heroes of the Ghetto

A gondola ride in Łazienki Park

ŁAZIENKI PALACE

The magnificent **Łazienki Palace and Garden Complex** (Łazienki Królewskie; ul. Agrykoli 1; gardens are free and open daily from dawn till dusk; Palace on the Isle Mon 11am–4pm, Tue–Sun 10am–4pm, longer hours in summer; www.lazienki-krolewskie.pl) is the former summer residence of King Stanisław August Poniatowski, Poland's final monarch. At the time of its completion in 1793, the so-called Palace on the Isle was far removed from the capital. Today, though, the 74-hectare (183-acre) park, opened to the public in 1818, lies right on the fringes of downtown Warsaw. The original 17th-century bathing pavilion was reshaped by the Italian architect Dominic Merlini into a magnificent Classical palace. Other buildings, including a theatre and the White House (Biały Dom) villa, along with several pavilions, orangeries, paths and canals, were added, transforming the complex into a handsome mixture of French classical and Baroque architecture and peaceful English-style gardens that are popular with locals.

In the main building, the Palace on the Isle, the neo-Classical Ballroom, Salamon Room and Art Gallery, which once displayed some 2,500 works of art (the most valuable of which were stolen or destroyed, though it still contains pieces from the collection of Stanisław August), are especially notable, as is the Dining Room, where the king held his celebrated 'Thursday dinners' with cultural and political figures. The Bacchus Room is decorated with original Delft tiles.

At the opposite end of the park, overlooking the Vistula Escarpment, is a recreation of the 1926 Secessionist **Monument to Frédéric Chopin**, depicting the composer under a willow tree, which is made to look like his piano-playing hand. The monument – which was reportedly the first destroyed by the Nazis – forms a popular outdoor venue for summer concerts.

WILANÓW

About 6km (4 miles) south of Łazienki is **Wilanów Palace** (Pałac w Wilanowie; ul. Potockiego 10–16, Wilanów; Palace: winter Wed–Mon 9.30am–3pm; Park: daily 9am till dusk; Thu free; summer Mon 9.30am–7pm, Tue, Thu, Fri 9.30am–3pm, Wed, Sat–Sun 9.30–5pm; opening hours might change so it's always better to check before going at www.wilanow-palac. pl), another royal summer residence, dating from 1679. Originally a grand old manor house, this Baroque gem was modelled on Versailles and surrounded by magnificent gardens. Villa Nova (which became 'Wilanów' in Polish) was the favourite spot of King John III Sobieski,

Chopin in summer

If you are visiting Warsaw in summer, visit the Monument to Frédéric Chopin on a Sunday afternoon, when concerts are held. The combination of the statue, lake and surrounding park create an ideal setting for Chopin's romantic music.

who saved Vienna from the Turks in 1683. After his death, Wilanów was passed among a long line of Polish aristocratic occupants, who altered and extended it. Wilanów was the last private residence nationalised by the new Communist government after World War II. The Czartoryski family, the noble family of art collectors that bequeathed their palace-museum to the city of Kraków, was one of the owners.

Even though many of the most valuable works of art were either stolen or destroyed, the palace, which didn't suffer great damage during World War II, still contains one of the largest collections of Polish portraits from the 16th to 19th centuries. The ground floor of the palace is the most opulent; the Great Crimson Room is a dining hall disguised as a painting gallery. After your tour, be sure to walk around the Italian gardens, noticing the palace's fine Baroque exterior decoration, the English-Chinese park, and the pond and Roman

Main gate at Wilanów Palace

bridge. Near the entrance to the palace grounds, somewhat incongruously, sits the **Poster Museum** (Muzeum Plakatu; ul. Potockiego 10–16, Wilanów; Mon noon–4pm, Tue–Sun 10am–4pm, free on Mon), dedicated to high-quality international poster art, a medium still highly respected today.

ŁÓDŹ

With approximately 707,000 inhabitants, **Łódź ❾** (pronounced 'woodge'), about 110km (70 miles) southwest of Warsaw, is the third-largest city in Poland, with light industry and about half of Polish textile production located within its boundaries. Łódź was granted a town charter as long ago as 1423, but in 1820 still only had 800 inhabitants. Things began to change in 1823 with the building of the New Town (Nowe Miasto), the first textile workers' estate. The removal of the customs barriers between Poland and Russia led to an enormous increase in the export of textiles to Russia, and in the late 19th century Łódź became one of the world's most important textile centres.

During World War II, the Germans opened two large transit camps in Łódź for Polish prisoners-of-war, as well as a camp for Russian airmen, a camp for 5,000 gypsies from Germany, Austria and the Balkans, and also a camp for 4,000 Polish children. Approximately 260,000 Jews were murdered in nearby Chełmno and Nerem, and the people of Łódź itself were also affected; of its 600,000 inhabitants only half survived the war.

After the war new housing and industrial estates grew up around the original districts of the town. In addition to the traditional textile industry, electrical engineering and chemical industries also came to Łódź, while in more recent times the city has begun to develop its cultural personality by encouraging the arts. The first institutions of further education were founded after the war, the most famous being the State

College of Cinematic Art, Drama and Television. The University of Łódź has a Department of Polish language for foreigners.

MAIN SIGHTS

Łódź's star attraction is ul. Piotrkowska, its huge, 5-km (3-mile) pedestrian street cutting the city neatly in two. Lined by some of the city's finest buildings, many of which house hotels, restaurants and bars, the summer sees the street come alive with scores of lively terraces scattered all the way down. Probably the most interesting project is Off Piotrowska (Piotrowska 138/140; entrance also from Roosevelt and Sienkiewicz streets; www.offpiotrkowska.pl), a restored former cotton mill now housing trendy workshops, galleries, shops and restaurants. The **Textile Museum** (Muzeum Włókiennictwa; ul. Piotrkowska 282; Mon closed, Tue–Wed and Fri 9am–5pm, Thur 11am–7pm, Sat–Sun 11am–4pm; permanent exhibitions free on Sat; www.muzeumwlokiennictwa.pl) is located here in the White Factory. It portrays the development of technology in the textile

ŁÓDŹ FILM SCHOOL

In his autobiography, Roman Polański writes: 'It was through a mere whim of history that Łódź became the film capital of Poland...after the war the capital, Warsaw, lay in ruins and...the government chose the nearest suitable town when looking for a place to establish a centre of cinematography.' Two years after World War II the Kraków film course transferred to Łódź and from then on it was here that filmmakers received their training. Polański, whose films include *Rosemary's Baby* and *Chinatown*, is probably the school's most celebrated director, but other alumni include director Andrzej Wajda *(The Promised Land, The Iron Man and Danton)* and Krzysztof Kieslowski *(The Double Life of Véronique, Three Colours: Blue, White, Red)*.

industry, and houses a fine collection of 16th-century to modern textiles from all over the world.

There are two further museums of note in the city. The **Museum of Art** (Muzeum Sztuki or ms1; ul. Więckowskiego 36; Tue 10am–6pm, Wed–Sun11am–7pm; www. msl.org.pl), in the palace once owned by the Poznański family, exhibits Polish and international art from the 19th century onwards. Other branches of the museum include ms2 (ul. Ogrodowa 19, same hours as ms1) – the old weaving factory, which houses

Piotrkowska Street, Łódź

an excellent collection of 20th and 21st century art and Herbst Palace (ul. Przędzalniana 72, Tue–Sun 11am–5pm).The Museum of the City of **Łódź** (Muzeum Miasta Łodzi; ul. Ogrodowa 15; Mon 10am–2pm, Tue 10am–4pm, Wed 2pm–6pm, Thur and Sat–Sun 11am–7pm; www.muzeum-lodz.pl), accommodated in another of the Poznańskis' palaces, documents the town's past, showing how it looked prior to World War II's devastation. Also on display is the memorabilia of Artur Rubinstein, the famous pianist and composer, who was born here. The excellent **Philharmonic Hall** of Łódź has been named after him.

Before the war, over 30 percent of the inhabitants of Łódź were Jewish. The Jewish community, both synagogues and the old Jewish cemetery were destroyed during the war. Only the new Jewish Cemetery (ul. Bracka 40), established in 1892, survived, with around 120,000 gravestones and the **Izrael Poznański Mausoleum** erected between 1903–5. Today it is allegedly the largest Jewish cemetery in Europe.

GDANSK

The northern city of **Gdańsk** ❿ catapulted to the world's attention as the focus of struggles between Polish workers and the Communist regime in the early 1980s. Images of the Gdańsk shipyards were beamed into living rooms around the world. The Solidarność, or Solidarity, workers' union not only helped set in motion a movement that would eventually topple governments throughout the Soviet Union, its leader, Lech Wałęsa – a shipyard electrician – became the first democratically elected president of post-Communist Poland in 1990.

Though Gdańsk's recent history has grabbed headlines, this city on the Baltic Sea has long been an important, and

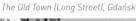
The Old Town (Long Street), Gdańsk

contentious, place. In 1308, the Teutonic Knights stormed the city, called Danzig by the Germans, and made it their medieval stronghold on the Baltic. It later became a prosperous port and trade centre as part of the Hanseatic League in the 14th century. For two centuries, the city essentially operated as an independent city-state. By the 16th century, Gdańsk was the largest city in Poland and the country's dominant international trade centre. During the Second Partition of Poland at the end of the 18th century, Prussia annexed the city; Napoleon laid siege to it in 1807 and declared it the Free City of Danzig; and the Congress of Vienna in 1815 returned it to Prussia.

Hitler began his acquisitive rampage here, and the assault on the Westerplatte peninsula on 1 September 1939 began World War II. The Old City, a spectacular creation of Gothic, Baroque and Renaissance architecture with a distinct Flemish aesthetic, was obliterated during the war. The city was meticulously rebuilt, and today it is one of the most spectacular of all of Poland's 'old cities'; its Royal Way is breathtaking, even though most of it was reconstructed in the 1950s. Amazingly, Gdańsk looks and feels like a 16th-century city.

Gdańsk is in fact the largest member of a Tri-city (Trójmiasto) region on the Baltic Sea. Gdańsk, Sopot and Gdynia form a 20km (12-mile) conurbation along the bay. While the three cities have retained their own distinct identities, Gdańsk is by far the most important and historic.

THE MAIN TOWN

Gdańsk is unusual among Polish cities. It has three distinct historic areas, but the Old Town is not in fact the birthplace of the city, and it doesn't possess the finest architectural ensemble. That distinction falls to the **Main Town** (Główne Miasto), often confused with the Old Town.

Golden Gate at night, Old Town, Gdańsk

THE ROYAL WAY

Gdańsk, despite its tortuous history of shifting allegiances, was loyal to the Polish crown for three centuries. When the king would travel from the capital, Warsaw, to the largest port (and provider of tax income), he would enter Gdańsk through a series of formal gates and down the extraordinary main thorough-fare. Kraków and Warsaw also have Royal Ways, but neither is as stunning as the one in Gdańsk. It is one of the undisputed highlights of Poland.

The king first passed through the brick **Upland Gate** (Brama Wyżynna), dating from the 16th century, where he was given the keys to the city. Beyond the Upland Gate is the **Golden Gate** (Złota Brama), a more ornamental structure formed by an arch topped by allegorical figures. The gate was added in 1614 but only recently fully restored to its original gilded splendour. Royal processions would then proceed onto **Long Lane** (ul. Długa), a pedestrian-only promenade lined with magnificent, brilliantly coloured three- and four-storey houses with fine Baroque portals, Gothic moldings, Renaissance façades, coats of arms and whimsical decorations. Most were rebuilt after World War II, which left the promenade in total ruins. A few original details did survive. Pause to admire house numbers 28, 29, 35 and 71. Of particular interest is **Uphagen's House** (Dom Uphagena; ul. Długa 12; Tue 10am–1pm, Wed–Sat 10am–4pm, till 6pm on Thu, Sun 11am–4pm; www.mhmg.pl), a museum occupying a splendid 18th-century merchant's house, with displays of textiles and rich period furnishings. Also at the same street, at 81/83, is The Second War Museum (Muzeum II Wojny Światowej; www.muzeum1939.pl; due to open in 2016) in a modern glass building.

At the end of ul. Długa is the 14th-century **Main Town Hall** (Tue 10am–1pm, Wed–Sat 10am–4pm, till 6pm on Thu, Sun 11am–4pm; www.mhmg.pl), crowned by a tall spire and life-size golden statue of King Sigismund August. The seat of the municipal government, it is one of the focal points of the Royal Way. The opulent interior, rich with oil paintings and frescoes, houses a branch of the **Gdańsk City History Museum** (Muzeum Historyczne Miasta Gdańska; for information on the city's museums see www.mhmg. pl), where you'll find a fine collection of photographs of the city before and after World War II. The fabulous Red Room, which once held Council debates, is all origi-nal; its decorative elements were dismantled and hidden during the war. Don't miss the views of the city from the top of the tower.

Just in front of the Town Hall is the **Neptune Fountain** (Fontanna Neptuna), a Flem-ish artist's beautiful bronze sculpture of the god of the sea, erected in 1633. It is said to be the oldest secular monument in Poland. Such was the locals' attachment to

Neptune Fountain, symbol of Gdańsk

the fountain that they dismantled it piece-by-piece and hid it during World War II, finally returning it to its original place in 1954. Neptune stands at the head of the second major section of the Royal promenade, **Long Market** (Długi Targ). Several of the most attractive houses in Gdańsk face the long market, which is more a boulevard than a square. Particularly impressive is the mansion **Artus Court** (Dwór Artusa; Długi Targ 43–4; Tue 10am–1pm, Wed–Sat 10am–4pm, till 6pm on Thu, Sun 11am–4pm, Free on Tue; www.mhmg.pl), a former meeting place for Gdańsk merchants, named after the court of King Arthur. Inside the massive hall, now a branch of the Gdańsk City History museum, is an immense mid-16th-century tiled stove, with a stunning assembly of more than 500 decorative tiles.

On the same side of the street is the **Golden House** (Złota Kamienica; Długi Targ 41–2), perhaps the most beautiful in the Old Town. The four-storey structure dates from the early 17th century. The magnificent (restored) façade is decorated with rich allegorical friezes, busts of historical figures, and at the top, four statues of gesticulating characters from classical mythology.

At the far end of Long Market is the **Green Gate** (Zielona Brama), a massive and bold, four-arched structure. More a building than a gate, it was intended to be a palace for visiting kings, though the exceedingly cold interior scared them away and no Polish monarch ever slept at the Green Gate.

Goldwasser

Gdańsk is famous as the birthplace of *Goldwasser* (gold water), which is vodka with added 23-carat gold leaf – once thought to have medicinal benefits. Whether the gold contributed to its flavour is a matter of opinion, but with this rich, sweet vodka, flavoured with a blend of herbs and spices, there is plenty to savour. Goldwasser was also renowned as the most expensive vodka, giving it added cachet.

WATERFRONT

Pass through the Green Gate and you'll discover the banks of the Motława River. To the right is the Gdansk Shakespeare Theatre (Teatr Szekspirowski, www.teatrszekspirowski.pl), a black brick building with a retractable roof, which holds the annual Gdansk Shakespeare Festival. To the left, is the **Great Crane** (Żuraw, ul. Szeroka 67–68; Tue–Sun 10am–3pm (winter) hours subject to change; check details at www.nmm.pl), is a giant gate built in 1444 to lift massive cargo onto ships and install ship masts.

Gdańsk waterfront

The crane now forms part of the sprawling **National Maritime Museum** (Narodowe Muzeum Morskie; ul. Ołowianka 9–13; Tue–Sun 10am–3pm (winter), longer in summer; www.nmm.pl), which expands across both sides of the river. Its buildings next to the Great Crane form the Maritime Culture Centre with a collection of antique shipping vessels and boats and exhibits documenting Polish and world seafaring history, including Swedish canons from the 17th-century Deluge. A boat shuttles visitors back and forth across the Motława river when it isn't frozen, and you can also step aboard the Sołdek, the first ocean-going vessel produced by the Gdańsk shipyards and launched in 1947.

Return to the interior of the city through **St Mary's Gate** (Brama Św. Marii), which leads to the quiet cobblestoned street, **ul. Mariacka**. It is one of the prettiest in Poland, with

Astronomical Clock at St Mary's

unique terraces and carved gargoyle drainpipes decorating every house. Like others in Gdańsk, this street was reconstructed after the war, but it lost none of its charm. Many of the houses are now jewellery shops specialising in amber, the local semi-precious stone (it's actually fossilised tree resin).

The street terminates in the red-brick Gothic **St Mary's Church** (Kościół Mariacki; ul. Podkramarska 5). The massive structure, begun in the 14th century but not finished until 150 years later, is one of the world's largest churches, said to be capable of holding up to 25,000 worshippers. Indeed, it is far more impressive for its sheer size than its exterior beauty. The Gothic vault interior retains 31 chapels, three dozen large windows and one amazing **astronomical clock**. The 15th-century clock features zodiac signs, phases of the moon, time and date, and a cast of characters that peep out to celebrate the tolling of the hour. Adam and Eve ring the bell, while the 12 apostles emerge from the right side. The story of the clock has a cruel twist: it is said that its maker's eyes were put out, by order of the mayor, so that he might never again build a clock to compete with it.

In the shadow of the St Mary's behemoth is the **Royal Chapel**, a small 17th-century Baroque Catholic church with a richly ornamented exterior. It is believed to be the work of

Tylman of Gameren, a Dutch architect. The dome-topped church was built for the city's then Catholic minority to comply with the will of the Primate of Poland. At the time, Gdańsk was a mainly Protestant city.

Just west of St Mary's (Targ Węglowy 6) is the landmark **Great Armoury**. Built in 1609 at the edge of the city's medieval walls, it is a huge Renaissance building with a spectacular façade, of marked Flemish influence. A great deal of work went into designing a building that would do little more than store armaments, and as such, it is also home to a shopping mall. The other side, which faces Targ Węglowy, is less ornate.

Wedged into a side street at the northern edge of the Main Town is **St Nicholas' Church** (Kościół Św. Mikołaja; ul. Świętojańska 72). Unlike much of the city, the Dominican church escaped major war damage. The light interior has a stunning collection of 10 black-and-gold Baroque altarpieces affixed to columns on either side of a central nave.

OLD TOWN

The **Old Town** (Stare Miasto) developed in tandem with the Main Town, though it was never as wealthy and after the war was not as lovingly or thoroughly rebuilt. Consequently, it has fewer sights of interest, but enough for a half-day's exploration.

Of principal interest is the **Great Mill** (Wielki Młyn; ul. Wielkie Młyny 16), a terrific structure with a sloping tiled roof. Built by the Teutonic Knights in 1350, the mill was the largest in medieval Europe, and it continued to function until the end of World War II. Today, however, it is an indoor shopping mall with all manner of clothing stores. Past the small pond behind the mill and across the street is Gdańsk's **Old Town Hall** (Ratusz Starego Miasta; ul. Korzenna 33–5; daily 10am–6pm), a 16th-century building that was labelled the pearl of the Dutch Renaissance. Designed by Antoon van Opberghen, who also designed the Great Armoury, this is where the town council met. It now contains a café and exhibition centre, but of greatest interest is the rich interior and the Great Hall.

Directly across the street from the Great Mill is **St Catherine's Church** (Kościół Św. Katarzyny; ul. Profesorska 3), the oldest church in Gdańsk, begun in 1220. The Gothic-vaulted interior is most celebrated for the enormous mural, on the left aisle depicting Christ's entry into Jerusalem. The church tower holds a 37-bell carillon that chimes on the hour and you can visit the interesting Tower Clock Museum (Mon–Wed and Fri–Sun 11am–7pm, Thu 10am–3pm; www.mhmg.pl)

Directly behind, or east of, St Catherine's is **St Bridget's Church** (Kościół Św. Brygidy; ul. Profesorska 17), which dates from the 15th century and later became a refuge for the Solidarity movement from the Communist government. Inside are several permanent displays related to the human rights struggles of the Polish workers' union. In fact, Lech Wałęsa attended Mass here before he became the spokes-man for Solidarność. The politicised nature of the church is evident on the right aisle in a series of crosses from the 1980s strikes, the gravestone of murdered priest (and Solidarność sympathizer) Jerzy Popiełuszko, and a bas-relief history of the workers' union.

A 10-minute walk north takes you to the old Gdańsk ship-yards, where the union protests took root. Today the ship-yard is being redeveloped and its former buildings are now trendy clubs like B90 (www.b90.pl). A huge **Monument of the Fallen Shipyard Workers** (Pomnik Poległych Stoczniowców; pl. Solidarności) commemorates the 44 who were killed in the 1970 street riots against the Communists. Nearby, is the strik-ing rust-coloured **European Centre of Solidarity** (Europejskie Centrum Solidarności; Plac Solidarności 1; daily 10am–6pm till 8pm in summer; www.ecs.gda.pl). It details the history of

Solidarity, and its excellent exhibition lays out the events that led to historic change in Eastern Europe. As well as the original demands of the 1980 shipyard strike, hand-written on plywood (now listed by Unesco) it gives visitors an insight into how hard life was in Communist times. From the top you can see a panorama of the historic areas of Gdańsk, including the shipyard.

OLD SUBURB

South of the Main Town is a third historic district, where the city expanded in the 15th century, now called the **Old Suburb** (Stare Przedmieście). Rebuilt after World War II, there are a couple of must-see sights here. The neighbourhood lies across the major road ul. Podwale Przedmiejskie.

Monument of the Fallen Shipyard Workers

The Gdańsk **National Museum** (Muzeum Narodowe; ul. Toruńska 1; May–Sep Tue–Sun 10am–5pm, Thu noon–7pm; Oct–Apr Tue–Fri 9am–4pm, Sat–Sun 10am –5pm; http://mng.gda.pl), with several branches across town, is one of Poland's most important repositories of medieval art, tapestries, embroidery, gold and silverware, all housed in a vaulted former Franciscan monastery and hospital. Its most famous work is The Last Judgement, a triptych by the 15th-century Dutch painter Hans Memling. The Flemish and Dutch collection also contain works by Van Dyck and Breughel the Younger.

Grand Hotel overlooking the beach, Baltic Coast

Abutting the museum is the **Church of the Holy Trinity** (Kościół Świętej Trójcy; ul. Św. Trójcy 4), Gdańsk's second-largest church. Built in the 15th century, the well-preserved Gothic structure has a spacious white interior. Of particular interest is the high altar, comprising varied panels in a triptych.

EXCURSIONS FROM GDANSK

Sopot ⓫, a former fishing village just 12km (7 miles) north of Gdańsk, is one of Poland's most fashionable seaside resorts. It began as a spa town in the 18th century and was little damaged by World War II. Sopot has a relaxed, elegant feel, complemented by the early 20th-century Secessionist buildings. The town attracts huge crowds of northern Europeans and Poles in the summer months, who are drawn in droves to the cafés, restaurants and nightclubs along the main pedestrian thoroughfare, ul. Bohaterów Monte Cassino, and to its sandy beaches and waters in the Gdańsk Bay. Sopot also has a 10-km (6-mile) path that runs through the park along the Baltic Sea, ideal for walking, running or cycling. Also popular are the promenade along the 1920s **pier** (Molo Południowe), Poland's longest, and the open-air **Forest Opera House** (Opera Leśna), a rather magical amphitheatre in the woods.

The next town north along the bay (some 21km/13 miles from Gdańsk), **Gdynia** ⓬, is also a former fishing village, although in the 20th century it was transformed into a large and wealthy industrial port city with boutiques, bars, restaurants and museums that draw visitors from across Poland. The majority of sights, clustered around the pier, are related to the sea and seafarers. Visit the ship museums (including the Błyskawica, a World War II destroyer, and Dar Pomorza, a 1909 three-masted frigate), or the **Aquarium** (Akwarium Gdyńskie; al. Jana Pawła II 1; daily (except occasional Mondays) Apr–May and Sept 9am–7pm; June 9am–8pm; Jul–Aug 9am–9pm; Oct–Mar 10am–5pm; www.akwarium.gdynia. pl), which includes exhibitions on oceanography, or visit the **Town Museum** (Muzeum Miasta Gdyni; ul. Zawiszy Czarnego 1; Tue,Wed, Fri 10am–6pm, Thu noon–8pm; www.muzeum gdynia.pl), which explains how Gdynia developed.

Both Sopot and Gdynia are easily reached by train (leaving every 10 minutes during the day, and less frequently late at night) from the Gdańsk Główny train station. It takes about 20 minutes to Sopot, and 30 minutes to Gdynia.

To escape the crowds, head to the tranquil **Hel Peninsula**, which stretches like a slim finger 35km (20 miles) across the bay. The string of fishing villages and sandy beaches is gaining in popularity as an easy day trip from Gdańsk, Sopot or Gdynia. Trains to Hel leave from Gdynia, and take 2 hours. For tourist information, see www.gohel.pl.

Alternatively, go inland to the unspoilt **Kashubia** (Kaszuby) region, a hilly land of folk art, an upside-down house and an ethnically distinct people with their own language and customs.

MALBORK CASTLE

Poland's largest, most famous castle is **Malbork** ⓭ (Zamek w Malborku; ul. Starościńska 1; Tue–Sun 10am–3pm, longer

Malbork Castle

in summer; www.zamek.malbork.pl), about 60km (37 miles) south of Gdańsk. The 14th-century medieval fortress, built by the Order of the Teutonic Knights on the banks of the River Nogat, gives every impression of being impregnable. It is a monumental red brick complex, with turrets, drawbridges and the most solid of walls dominating the flat plains that lie around it.

In 1280, the Teutonic Knights built a fortified monastery, and in 1308, the Grand Master came to live in Malbork, elevating the status of the settlement to headquarters of the entire Order. The interior of the castle is astounding, a labyrinth of seemingly unending rooms and chapels. Highlights include the perfectly harmonious vaulting in the refectory, the stunning Gothic portal known as the Golden Gate, the massive Knight's Hall and the museum collection of amber. Even after the defeat and retreat of the Teutonic Knights, the castle never fell into ruin. Indeed it became a residence of the Polish monarchs.

Inclusive visits are by guided tour only, though some parts of the castle complex can be visited on one's own. Getting to Malbork is straightforward. The train journey from Gdańsk Główny train station takes 40 minutes by express train or an hour by regular train. From Malbork town, the castle is an easy 10-minute walk. This impressive landmark is well worth the time.

During summer months, Malbork Castle stages hour-long evening sound-and-light shows in the main courtyard.

TORUN

In the lower Vistula Valley, 182km (113 miles) south of Gdańsk, lies the handsome, historic city of **Toruń ⑭**. Founded by the Teutonic Knights in 1233, the medieval walled town sits on the right bank of Poland's greatest river. It's probably best known, however, as the birthplace of Mikołaj Kopernik – or, as most people know him, Nicolaus Copernicus, the great 16th-century astronomer.

Toruń's city council outlawed wooden buildings in the 14th century, requiring all the city's important edifices to be made of brick and stone. At the time, the city won accolades as 'beautiful red Toruń'. With a unique collection of Gothic architecture, including a ruined castle, fine churches, fortifications, a leaning tower and the home of Copernicus, Toruń is a Unesco World Heritage Site. The town is easily covered on foot, with a day's walking tour taking in all the sights (allow longer to visit the museums).

OLD TOWN

The core of the city's **Old Town** (Stare Miasto) is its

Toruń gingerbread

Toruń is known for its traditional gingerbread, and its bakers can be pretty creative with the medieval recipe. Look for gingerbread figures of Copernicus, among other fancy creations.

Old Town Square (Rynek Staromiejski). In its middle stands the dignified **Town Hall** (Ratusz), a solid Gothic brick construction raised in the 14th century, with Dutch Renaissance turrets and gables (the clock tower, formerly an independent structure, was built in 1247). Suitable for a town known for a mathematician-astronomer, the Town Hall has 12 halls representing the months of the year, 52 small rooms representing the number of weeks, and 365 windows for each day of the year. The former municipal seat of government has been almost wholly taken over by the **Regional Museum** (Muzeum Okręgowe; Rynek Staromiejski 1; Oct–Apr Tue–Sun 10am–4pm; May–Sept 10am–6pm; free on Wed; www.muzeum.torun.pl), which displays a fine collection of Gothic art, stained glass and Polish painting amid Gothic interiors with vaulted ceilings. The top of the clock tower affords a sweeping view of Toruń's red-tile roofs and the river.

Toruń's Old Town

In the southeast corner of the square, in front of the Town Hall, is a statue commemorating Toruń's most famous citizen, and much revered Pole **Nicolaus Copernicus**. Across the street is a large, extravagant 19th-century building known as **Arthur's Court** (Dwór Artusa; Rynek Staromiejski 6), formerly a meeting place for town merchants and today the site of a cultural centre. Facing the square on its east side is a pretty yellow four-storey building with an ornate Baroque façade and gabled roof. Called the **House Under the Star** (Kamienica Pod Gwiazda; Rynek Staromiejski 35; Oct–Apr Tue–Sun 10am–4pm; May–Sept 10am–6pm; free on Wed; www.muzeum.torun.pl), it's a museum displaying art from the Far East.

On the opposite side of the Rynek is the uninspiring 18th-century **Church of the Holy Spirit** (Kościół pw. Ducha Świętego). Between it and the Town Hall is a fountain featuring a slew of frogs and a young boy playing the violin. It represents a legend that says Toruń was once invaded by frogs and the boy charmed them back to the woods with his violin. Just off the northwest corner of the square is the imposing **St Mary's Church** (Kościół Mariacki), a Franciscan monastery from the 13th century.

Around the corner to the north is Toruń's **Planetarium** (Planetarium Centrum Popularyzacji Kosmosu; ul. Franciszkańska 15–21; charge; www.planetarium.torun.pl, see website for show times). Installed in a 19th-century gasworks, whose round shape was perfect for its needs. There are a variety of different shows available daily. Across the street is Toruń's respected Mikołaj Kopernik University, also a feast of Gothic brick.

Toruń's other major sights are south of the Rynek. The **House of Nicholas Copernicus** (Dom Mikołaja Kopernika; ul. Kopernika 15–17; Oct–Apr Tue–Sun 10am–4pm; May–Sept 10am–6pm;

free on Wed, www.muzeum.torun.pl), inhabits the handsome burgher's house where the astronomer was born in 1473.

Directly south of the museum, along ul. Bankowa, are remnants of the city's fortifications, of which four bastions and three gates still survive. Nearby are old granaries, the Monastery Gate and the **Leaning Tower** (Krzywa Wieża; Pod Krzywą Wieżą). The towers structural flaw is explained away by a legend that states that a Teutonic Knight, a monk sworn to chastity, was caught *in flagrante* with a townswoman and made to build a leaning tower to show the harm of deviance from upright moral standards.

COPERNICUS

One of the world's most influential astronomers, Mikołaj Kopernik (Nicolaus Copernicus, 1473–1543) was born in Toruń, the son of a prosperous merchant. The house in which Copernicus was born is now a museum detailing his life and works and houses the original edition of *De Revolutionibus Orbium Coelestium*, his revolutionary, initially very controversial, theory that the sun, not the earth, was the centre of the universe.

Copernicus is said to have studied at the Jagiellonian University in Kraków. In 1497 he went to Italy to continue his studies; it was there that he witnessed a lunar eclipse, which first led him to question whether the earth was the centre of the universe. It was not until 1543, however, that his book on the subject was published, in Nuremberg. Copernicus – who only saw a copy as he lay dying of a brain haemorrhage – dedicated the book to Pope Paul III, but the Roman Catholic Church still considered his theories to be 'subversive', and the work was banned until 1757. Yet it provided a basis for subsequent theories by distinguished astronomers including Galileo. The argument over whether Copernicus was actually Polish or German is expected to continue until the universe he first described is no more.

On the corner of ul. Żeglar-ska and ul. Św. Jana is Toruń's largest church, the 13th-century **Cathedral of Saints John the Baptist and John the Evangelist** (Katedra Św. Janów, www.katedratorun.pl). Before going in, note the clock on the southern side; added in the 15th century, it still works today. The spacious interior has Gothic vaulting and a series of attractive chapels and altars. Some frescoes have been uncovered; the most interesting is the mono-chrome painting of the devil high at the back of the right aisle. A chapel nearby holds a medieval font in which Copernicus was baptised.

Copernicus Monument

East of the cathedral are the ruins of the **Teutonic Castle**, built by the Order in the 13th century. Toruń citizens destroyed it in 1454 (and hounded the Order out of town) and it has lain in ruins since. There is just one surviving tower and a covered passageway you can walk through.

NEW TOWN

In contrast to the Old Town, the buildings in the expansion east were built mostly of wood. They didn't survive, so what remain in the New Town (Nowe Miasto) are mainly brick constructions of the 15th and 16th centuries. The **New Town Square** (Rynek Nowomiejski) is less impressive than its older counterpart, but worth a look. The major church in this part of town is **St James's**

Bleat the clock

Crowds gather daily at noon beneath the tower of the Town Hall to see two mechanical billy goats emerge from the parapet in the clock tower. A 16th-century tradition, the metal goats butt horns 12 times to signal the hour.

Church (Kościół Św. Jakuba; Rynek Nowomiejski 6), which dates from 1309 and is notable for its flying buttresses. Inside are some interesting Gothic wall paintings.

Walk west to Plac Teatralny, at the edge of the Old Town, where you'll find Toruń's major theatre, the neo-Baroque **Teatr Horzycy** (Plac Teatralny 1). The park across the intersection holds a very interesting *skansen*, or outdoor **Ethnographic Museum** (Muzeum Etnograficzne; ul. Wały gen. Sikorskiego 19; Oct–mid-Apr Tue–Fri 9am–4pm, Sat–Sun 10am–4pm; mid-Apr–June Tue and Thur 9am–5pm, Wed and Fri 9am–4pm, Sat–Sun 10am–6pm; July–Sept Wed and Fri 9am–4pm, Tue, Thur, Sat and Sun 10am–6pm; www.etnomuzeum.pl). Dating from 1959, it displays a collection of 18th- to early-20th-century houses. Once a year, on a Sunday in September, the *skansen* becomes a living museum with actors playing the parts of blacksmiths and other rural workers.

POZNAN

Halfway between Berlin and Warsaw, **Poznań** ⓯ is the principal city of Wielkopolska, a region in western Poland that is one of the country's largest and most historic. Wielkopolska means Great Poland, a title that reflects its role in the development of the Polish nation. Wielkopolska is effectively the birthplace of Poland: in the 10th century, Prince Mieszko succeeded in uniting the Polanie (literally, 'people of the fields') and neighbouring Slavic tribes, founding the Polish state in 966.

Until the royals adopted Kraków in 1038, Poznań was in essence the capital of Poland. The city began its development on the island of Ostrów Tumski and the new town centre was begun in the 13th century. In the 18th century, it fell to the Prussians under the Second Partition and became increasingly Germanic, a trait for which it is still known today. In modern times, Poznań is best known for a tragic episode: in 1956, a workers' strike was crushed by the Communist government, leaving at least 76 people dead and nearly 1,000 injured.

Today Poznań is one of the most dynamic and prosperous cities in Poland, with an attractive historic core, a wealth of Gothic, Renaissance and neo-Classical architecture, and a civic commitment to business development and international trade. Poznań draws large numbers of business visitors, but the city also enchants tourists, who concentrate on three primary areas: the Stary Rynek, or Old Market Square, the Ostrów Tumski island and the New Town (Nowe Miasto).

Castle ruins, Toruń

OLD MARKET SQUARE

In Poznań you will find the **Old Market Square** (Stary Rynek), one of the largest and finest in Poland. The fairytale **Town Hall** (Ratusz), a fanciful construction of Italian Renaissance designed by Giovanni Battista di Quadro. The building, constructed in the 1550s, features a splendid three-storey Renaissance, arcaded loggia and a classical tower, added in 1783, topped by the Polish eagle. The brilliant colours of the frieze above the loggia, depicting the Jagiellonian dynasty kings, have been restored to their original splendour, returning the building to its status as one of the most distinctive in Poland. Although part of that status might derive from the mechanical fighting goats which clash daily over the clock. Adding to the sites of interest, just in front of the Town Hall is a copy of a 1535 pillory, with a Rococo **Proserpina Fountain** dating from the 18th century.

The Town Hall holds the **History Museum of Poznań** (Muzeum Historii Miasta Poznania; Stary Rynek 1; Tue–Thur 9am–3pm, mid-June–mid-Sept 11am–5pm, Fri noon–9pm, Sat–Sun 11am–6pm, Sun 10am–3pm; www.mnp.art.pl). The Great Hall is a spectacular vaulted room with a Renaissance ceiling, rich with stucco decoration, coats of arms, symbols of the heavens and exotic animals. The museum displays a collection of art, medieval sculpture, distinctive 'coffin

Musical interlude

The Museum of Musical Instruments (Muzeum Instrumentów Muzycznych; Stary Rynek 45-7; Tue–Thur 9am–3pm and 11am–5pm mid-June–mid-Sept, Fri noon–9pm, Sat–Sun 11am–6pm; www.mnp.art.pl) is the only one of its kind in Poland. Inside you'll find early phonographs, church and Polish-army drums, a Celtic horn, 17th-century Polish violins from Groblicz, and a pianoforte once played by Chopin, as well as odd Polish folk instruments and exotic drums from around the world.

Poznań's Old Market Square

portraits' (paintings of the deceased attached to their caskets)
and Poznań crafts from the 10th to the mid-20th century. In the
Court Chamber, there are frescoes representing the four conti-
nents then known – Europe, Asia, Africa and America.

Adjoining the Town Hall to the south is a row of narrow and
colourful fish sellers' houses, built in the 1500s. Lining the four
sides of the square are elegant and colourful arcaded burgh-
ers' houses and two magnificent palaces. Many remarkable
edifices had to be rebuilt in the 1950s, following World War
II, to their original Gothic, Baroque and Renaissance designs.
Almost all of the Rynek's houses have vaulted medieval cellars, several of which have been converted into atmospheric
restaurants. Some of the best preserved include No. 37, today
the Maison de la Bretagne (Dom Bretanii), but formerly the oldest pharmacy in Poznań – and No.s 40, 41, 42 and 43. A pharmacy, established at no 41 in 1564, the White Eagle, only moved
at the end of the 20th century. On the façade of the **Henryk
Sienkiewicz Literature Museum** (Muzeum Literackie Henryka

Town Hall

Sienkiewicza; Stary Rynek 84; Tue–Fri 9am–5pm, Sat 9am–4pm, free on Sat; www.bracz.edu.pl), devoted to the Polish Nobel-prizewinning writer, you'll see a statue of the Italian architect, Battista di Quadro, who lived here.

The 18th-century **Działyński Palace**, (www.bkpan.poznan.pl) at the corner of ul. Franciszkańska on the west side of the square, is a lovely classical structure painted a light shade of green and decorated with sculptures and reliefs. On top is a pelican, symbolic of Poznań's rebirth after the Partition of Poland. More spectacular than the façade is the Red Room, where 'literary Thursdays' were held in the period between the World Wars. The palace at No. 91 belonged to the Mielżyński family.

The middle of the square is also occupied by a large, incongruous and unattractive 1950s- and 1960s-era pavilion, which was constructed after the war on the sites of the old cloth hall and arsenal, and houses the **Galeria Miejska Arsenał** contemporary art gallery (Stary Rynek 3; Tue noon–7pm, Wed–Sat 1–8pm, Sun noon–4pm; www.arsenal.art.pl). The building mars the otherwise exquisite harmony of the square.

In a passageway between the pavilion and Town Hall is the **Monument of a Bamberg Woman** in folkloric dress on the way to a well, with large jugs in both hands. The statue pays tribute to 18th-century immigrants to Poznań from

Bamberg, Germany. One of Poznań's most stately residences is the **Górka Palace**, built in the mid-16th century and occupying an entire block on the corner of Wodna and Świętosławska streets (southeast corner of the Stary Rynek). Note the Renaissance portals; in the interior is a beautiful arcaded courtyard. The palace passed from the Górkas, one of Poznań's most powerful families, to Benedictine nuns during the Reformation; today it is the site of the **Archaeological Museum** (Muzeum Archeologiczne; ul. Wodna 27; Sept–June Tue–Thur 9am–4pm Fri–Sat 10am–5pm, Sun noon–4pm; July–Aug Tue–Thur 10am–4pm Fri noon–7pm, Sat 11am–7pm, Sun noon–5pm; free on Sat; www.muzarp.poznan.pl), displaying a collection of artefacts dating to the prehistory and foundations of Wielkopolska as well as ancient Egypt. New excavations and restoration are ongoing at the site.

During the summer, the Stary Rynek is full of lively outdoor cafés, and concerts and performances are frequently staged here. At night the square is beautifully illuminated and a wonderful place to take a stroll.

AROUND OLD MARKET SQUARE

A block south of Górka Palace is Poznań's stunning salmon-coloured **Parish Church of St Stanislaus** (Kościół Św. Stanisława; ul. Gołębia 1). A Jesuit church until 1701, it is one of the most important Roman Baroque churches in Poland. Note the curious flat cupola that is in fact an optical illusion, giving the impression of being a dome.

Adjoining the Parish Church, the handsome orange-pink collection of buildings, formerly the Jesuit College, now house Poznań's municipal government.

West of the Old Market Square are several places of interest. The Baroque **Franciscan Church** (Kościół św. Antoniego z Padwy; ul. Franciszkańska 2), with its twin towers, dates from the first half of the 18th century. Across ul. Franciszkańska is the **Museum of Applied Arts** (Muzeum Sztuk Użytkowych; ul. Góra Przemysła 1; closed), housed inside the remains of the city's former royal castle, continually destroyed and rebuilt. The present buildingis a reconstruction from the 18th century.

CITY CENTRE

Further west is the main building of the **National Museum** (Muzeum Narodowe; al. Marcinkowskiego 9; Tue–Thur 9am–3pm, 11am–5pm mid-June–mid-Sept, Fri noon–9pm, Sat–Sun 11am–6pm; www.mnp.art.pl), facing Plac Wolności (Freedom Square) – which ought to be called Bank Square, given the preponderance of Polish and foreign banks here. The main building of the museum is the older one, built at the begin-ning of the 20th century and modelled on the Berlin Arsenal. The collection of medieval art, 16th- to 18th-century European

Parish Church of St Stanislaus

painting – featuring Spanish and Flemish Old Masters – and contemporary Polish art by artists including Malczewski, Matejko and Wyspiański, is quite impressive.

Also on Freedom Square, at no 19, is the **Raczyński Library**, commissioned in the early 19th century and modelled on the Musée du Louvre in Paris. It is one of Poland's oldest public libraries.

Architecture from the days of Prussian control of Poznań can be found west of Freedom Square. Look for the colonnaded **Grand Theatre** (Teatr Wielki; ul. Fredry 9), with a classical portico, and the neo-Renaissance **Collegium Minus** of the university. In front of the university is a **Monument to the Victims of Poznań, June 1956**, whose two crosses mourn the protesting workers who were killed during violent demonstrations against the Communist government.

Across the street is the monolithic **Kaiserhaus**, also called 'the castle' by locals, constructed for the German Emperor Wilhelm II (he never once came to spend the night here). The massive structure now holds the Cultural Centre Zamek (http://zamek.poznan.pl) with interesting temporary exhbitions. Also of note is the **June 1956 Poznań Uprising Museum** (Muzeum Powstania Poznańskiego – Czerwiec 1956; ul. Św. Marcina 80–2; Tue–Fri 9am–5pm, Sat–Sun 10am–4pm; free on Fri, www.muzeumniepodleglosci.poznan.pl), a small but poignant museum portraying the days of unrest in the city during that year.

Directly west of here are Poznań's international fair grounds, which date from the 1920s and are the biggest and busiest in Poland.

CATHEDRAL ISLAND

Poznań has its origins on the tranquil little **Cathedral Island** (Ostrów Tumski), surrounded by the rivers Cybina and Warta and only a 15-minute walk east from the Old Market Square. Indeed, as the late Pope John Paul II once said, the island – today a hushed ecclesiastical district – is 'where Poland began'. Near the river Cybina at Gdańska 2 is the architecturally acclaimed **ICHOT Gate** (Brama Poznania ICHOT, www. bramapoznania.pl; Tue–Fri 9am–6pm; Sat–Sun 10am–7pm), which has an interactive centre of the history of Ostrów Tumski.

The island's crowning glory is its **Cathedral** (Katedra; Ostrów Tumski 17). At the beginning of the 9th century, the Piast Dynasty built a settlement and castle on the island. The actual foundations of the pre-Polish state are beneath the Cathedral, the oldest landmark on the island, dating back to 968. The main part of the church is Gothic, from the 14th and 15th centuries (the roof, twin towers and most of the interior were destroyed during World War II). On the left rear of the altar is the **Golden Chapel** (Złota Kaplica), a riot of ornate

Ostrów Tomski, Cathedral Island

gold decoration from the
first half of the 19th century, built as a mausoleum
for the two rulers who were
instrumental in building the
Polish state, Mieszko I and
his son, Bolesław the Brave.
The chapel on the right aisle
has fine 1616 frescoes on
the arches; in the right rear,

> **Croissant crazy**
>
> Poznań is famous for its
> celebrations on 11 November
> honouring the 4th-century
> St Martin. On that day only
> Poznanians gobble up St
> Martin croissants, in the
> shape of buffalo horns,
> stuffed with poppy seeds.

the Royal Chapel features an epitaph to the last king buried in Poznań (all of the others were subsequently buried in
Kraków). The Chapel of the Holy Sacrament holds the impressive Renaissance tomb of the Górka family. In the Cathedral
crypt are the ancient foundations of the first church on this
site, excavated in the 1950s, and an archaeological museum.
Next to the cathedral is the **Archaeological Reserve Genius
Loci** (Rezerwat Archeologiczny Genius Loci; www.muzarp.
poznan.pl; Tue–Thu 10am–4pm, Sun 10am–3pm, Apr–Sep
Fri noon–7pm, Sat 11am–7pm; Oct–Mar Fri 11am–6pm, Sat
9am–5pm) that shows archaeological remains of the earliest
settlements in Ostrów Tumski.

MALTA

For leisure and sport, head to **Malta** – a lake and park district east of the Old Town. Lake Maltańskie is an artificial lake
constructed in the 1950s, where there are frequent regattas,
a beach and water sports, in addition to a year-round man-
made ski slope and a summer toboggan run. The path around
the lake is popular with runners and cyclists. Concerts and
theatre performances are held in summer, and there are
some good restaurants and one of Poznań's best hotels on
the shores of the lake.

EXCURSIONS FROM POZNAN

Two popular side trips from Poznań are to a castle and palace in the towns of Kórnik and Rogalin, respectively. Both can be visited by bus from Poznań, and you can go first to Kórnik and then on to Rogalin without having to go back to Poznań first.

KÓRNIK CASTLE

Kórnik Castle (Zamek w Kórniku; Mar–mid-Dec Tue–Sun 10am–4pm; www.bkpan.poznan.pl), about 20km (12 miles) to the southeast, was built by one of Poznań's richest, most powerful families, the Górkas, in the 15th century. The castle's modified appearance both inside and out was effected under the ownership of another important family, the Działyńskis, in the 1800s. The castle houses their collections of art and military regalia, as well as their original furnishings. Beautiful hardwood floors and carved wood portals are found throughout. The most surprising aspect is the Moorish Hall, based on the Alhambra in Granada, Spain. The castle grounds were established as an arboretum in the 19th century, with over 2,500 species of plants and trees.

ROGALIN PALACE

Rogalin Palace, 13km (8 miles) west of Kórnik (May–Nov Tue–Sun 10am–5pm, winter till 4pm; http://rogalin.mnp.art.pl). The renovated 18th-century Baroque palace of Kazimierz Raczyński, the secretary of the king, it is noteworthy for its gardens and small museum. The right wing of the museum holds portraits of the Raczyński family and a mock-up of the London apartment of Edward, a diplomat. Off to the left of the main house is a gallery of 'salon paintings'. In the attractive English-style gardens are three massive oak trees, each about 600 years old. The trees were named after three dukes – Lech, Czech and Rus – who founded the Polish, Czech and Russian nations.

WROCŁAW

South of Poznań surrounded by the scenic beauty of the Lower Silesian countryside lies the city of **Wrocław** 16. The most important city in Silesia and the European Capital of Culture in 2016. Arrival by train makes a good first impression: the late 19th century neo-Gothic white stucco station houses a main hall that is 200 metres (650ft) long, built as one of the largest stations in Central and Eastern Europe.

Rogalin Palace

OSTRÓW TUMSKI

Starting on Cathedral Island or Ostrów Tumski, you'll be able to visit several churches, the most important being the **Cathedral of St John the Baptist** (Katedra Św Jana Chrzciciela; Mon-Sat 10am-4.30pm, Sun 2-4pm), dating from the 13th century. The cathedral also offers excellent views over the city. From here, cross over **Cathedral Bridge** (Most Tumski) which displays figures of St Hedwig and John the Baptist and links Cathedral Island with the Old Town.

THE OLD TOWN

With a monumental white Baroque façade, dating from 1811, Collegium Maximum forms the main building of the **University** (Uniwersytet). Situated on the leafy banks overlooking the pretty **River Odra** (Oder), it was established on the site of a medieval castle which guarded the ford across the river. The interiors are all eclipsed by the magnificent Leopoldine Hall (pl Uniwersytecki 1; Sep–Apr Thu–Tue 10am–3.30pm, May–Aug Mon, Tue,Thu 10am–4pm, Fri–Sun 10am–5pm). One of Poland's most beautiful Baroque halls. Other halls worth visiting include the Oratorium, Marianum and the Mathematical Tower (opening hours as above), offering a superb view over the city.

Nearby is the **Baroque Ossoliński Library** (Biblioteka Ossolińskich; tel: 071-344 44 71). Its collection of illuminated manuscripts includes the Florentine publication of **Dante's Divine Comedy of 1481**. Passing the 19th-century red brick **Covered Market** (Hala Targowa), formerly a tram depot, you can head to the **National Museum** (Muzeum Narodowe; pl Powstanc.w Warszawy 5; www.mnwr.art.pl; Apr–Sept Wed–Fri and Sun 10am–5pm, Sat 10am–6pm, Oct–Mar Wed–Fri 10am–4pm, Sat–Sun 10am–5pm). It houses an extensive collection of Silesian, Gothic and Polish art.

Along the banks of the Oder River, Wrocław

A stroll across **Słowacki Park** (Park J. Słowackiego) leads to a modern rotunda. It houses the city's most popular tourist attraction, the **Panorama of the Battle of Racławice** (Panorama Racławicka; Purkiniego 11; www.panoramaraclacwicka. pl; mid-Apr–Sept daily 9am–5pm, Oct Tue–Sun 9am–5pm, Nov–mid-Apr Tue–Sun 9am–4pm). Climb the circular staircase to the dome, where a painting depicting the battle won against Russian forces in 1793 will take your breath away.

AROUND THE MARKET SQUARE

In the centre of the **Old Town** (Stare Miasto) is the fine Gothic **Town Hall** (Ratusz). The **Museum of Bourgeois Art** (Muzeum Sztuki Mieszczańskiej; ul Sukiennice 14/15; Wed–Sat 10am–5pm, Sun 10am–6pm) is on the Town Hall's upper floors, while the 15th-century cellar, Piwnica Świdnicka, serves local beers. The **Market Square** (Rynek) is extraordinary, for the range of architectural styles found here, with Gothic, Renaissance and neo-Gothic styles all within a few feet of one another.

For a change of scene, leave from the southwest corner onto Plac Solny and make your way onto **Świdnicka**, the city's main shopping thoroughfare. Here you will also find the elegant neoclassical **Opera House** (www.opera.wroclaw.pl) and the **Historical Museum** (Muzeum Historyczne; Kazimierza Wielkiego 35; www.muzeum.miejskie.wroclaw.pl; Tue–Fri 10am–5pm, Sat–Sun 10am–6pm). Its permanent '1,000 Years of Wrocław' exhibition is worthy of a look.

Across the **Odra** (Oder) River in **Śródmieście** (Middletown) is the historic Centennial Hall (Hala Stulecia). Inside is the cutting edge **Discovery Centre** (Centrum Poznawcze; http://centrum poznawcze.pl; Apr–Oct Sun–Thu 9am–6pm, Fri–Sat 9am–7pm, Nov–Mar daily 9am–5pm). Close by is the **Zoological Garden** (Wróblewskiego 1-5; www.zoo.wroclaw.pl), the largest and most popular zoo in the country.

WHAT TO DO

From markets stalls and shopping malls to folk bands and opera, Poland offers plenty of shopping and entertainment opportunities to suit all tastes and budgets. Come sundown, the country doesn't disappoint either with a wealth of pubs, bars, clubs and live music venues in every major city.

SHOPPING

The demise of Communism in 1989 and the move to a free-market economy have had a dramatic impact on Poland as a shopping destination. Drab state-owned stores are a thing of the past. The pound, dollar, euro and other currencies don't go as far today as they once did, but foreign visitors and their Polish counterparts can only be pleased with the opening of trade and vastly improved selection of goods on the market. In major cities like Warsaw and Kraków, Poland doesn't lag far behind Western Europe and North America for commercial opportunities and you will find branches of many of the global chains here. Even with the end of Communism and inflation, Poland remains considerably cheaper than Western European destinations.

WHERE TO SHOP

Poland's development of a market economy has produced a proliferation of stores and boutiques, including many imports from Western Europe and North America that can be found in modern department stores, speciality shops and market stalls.

The price is right

Note that the price displayed is the price that is expected to be paid – it is not the done thing to haggle in Polish shops.

Skiing in Zieleniec

Baltic amber for sale in Gdańsk

For folk art and other handicrafts, start at branches of Cepelia (http://cepelia.pl) stores, a national chain of folk art and souvenir shops in large cities. (Occasionally, they go by different names, even though locals invariably call them Cepelia.) For antiques, the dominant player is the Desa (www.desa.pl) chain (though there are many smaller, independent dealers as well). Poland has a rich and thriving tradition of graphic art and the best places in the country to look for Polish posters are: in Kraków, Galeria Plakatu Kraków (ul. Stolarska 8–10; www.cracowpostergallery.com); and in Warsaw, Galeria Polskiego Plakatu (Rynek Starego Miasta 23; www.poster.com.pl); Galeria Grafiki i Plakatu (ul. Hoża 40; www.galeriagrafikiiplakatu.pl) and the Poster Museum (Muzeum Plakatu; www.postermuseum.pl) at Wilanów Palace.

Speciality shopping markets include the unmissable **Cloth Hall stalls**, loaded with crafts and amber jewellery, in Kraków, whose history is as long as the city's; Warsaw's swanky, boutique-lined **ul. Nowy Świat**; and **ul. Mariacka** in Gdańsk's Main Town for amber jewellery. An interesting open-air market in Warsaw is the Koło Bazaar, in Wola. In Kraków, the best flea markets are on Sunday mornings in Plac Nowy in Kazimierz and next to Hala Targowa on ul.

Grzegórzecka. In Gdańsk, the covered market (Hala Targowa) is at pl. Dominikański 1.

Good sources for local shops and markets in Warsaw, Kraków and Gdańsk are the local editions of the In Your Pocket guide, which features individual store listings. See www.inyourpocket.com for more information.

Bargaining is generally only acceptable at the large **open-air markets**, though if you ask for a discount at an antiques store or art gallery, you may well be granted one.

WHAT TO BUY

Art and antiques. You'll find excellent antique furnishings and religious art throughout Poland, though the best pieces tend to wind up in the wide spectrum of shops and galleries in Warsaw and Kraków, and to a lesser extent cities like Gdańsk and Poznań. Religious icons from the Orthodox Church in Russia can be found, as a large black market in stolen icons exists throughout Central and Eastern Europe, although officials are understandably touchy about their export, even when the item in question is not originally from Poland. Strict export restrictions apply, see Visas and entry requirements, page 179.

AMBER

This attractive fossilised tree resin (not a semi-precious stone) is available in many shades, from yellow to brown, and grades of clarity. The cities near the Baltic Sea, Gdańsk and Gdynia, have an abundance of amber and excellent shops, often dealing in unique pieces. Be careful not to buy amber on the street, as it is likely to be fake; look for a sign of the Amber Association of Poland ('Societas Succinorum in Polonia', www.amber.org.pl) in shop windows as a guarantee of quality and authenticity.

Painted wooden eggs, a typical Polish souvenir

Ceramics and pottery. Distinctive Kashubian pottery known as Ceramika Artystyczna Bolesławiec is sold the world over but is considerably cheaper in Poland.

Folk art. Rustic Poland excels at folk art and handicrafts, including hand-carved wooden (usually religious) figures; leather goods from the Tatra Mountains; embroidery and lace; hand-painted eggs (especially at Easter); and colourful naïve art and glass paintings, especially from Zakopane.

Music. CDs from Polish composers are available in record shops in major cities. The most recognisable to Western listeners are probably composers Frédéric Chopin, Krzysztof Penderecki and Henryk Górecki, who unexpectedly scored an international best seller with his Symphony No. 3 in the early 1990s. A contemporary film composer, Zbigniew Preisner, who wrote the scores for the Polish director Krzysztof Kieślowski's films, including *The Double Life of Veronique*, *Dekalogue* and the *Three Colours trilogy: Red, White and Blue*, is worth seeking out. Of special note is a recording of the best of Preisner recorded live in the Wieliczka Salt Mines outside Kraków. You can also find recordings of Polish folk music, such as traditional *górale*, or highlander, tunes from the Tatras.

Poster art. Poster design is a thriving and valued art form in Poland, and some of the finest poster artists in the world are Polish. You'll find vintage and contemporary posters for familiar Western films and the greatest hits of theatre and opera, as well as more obscure titles. Contemporary poster designers include Górowski, Stasys (Stasys Eidrigevicius), Andrzej Pągowski, Rafał Olbiński and Wiktor Sadowski.

Vodka. For an authentic bottle of Polish vodka, or wódka (pronounced 'voot-ka'), look for Wyborowa, Extra Żytnia or any flavoured vodka, such as Żubrówka (with a blade of bison grass in the bottle) and Wiśniówka (cherry-flavoured).

ENTERTAINMENT

Nightlife in Warsaw and Kraków is very cosmopolitan, with a full range of cultural offerings, including theatre, opera, ballet and classical music. In other cities, there is less variety, though both Gdańsk and Poznań have lively programmes of fine arts. Tickets for performances are much more accessibly priced than in most of Western Europe or North America.

On the pop culture front, you'll find jazz combos and films from around the world. Big-name international pop and rock bands are now routinely including Poland in their touring schedules. You'll find a range of bars, pubs, cafés and nightclubs in the cities, as well as a handful of casinos.

Performing arts. In the principal cities, Poles are stalwart supporters of the performing arts. In Warsaw, the Great

In your pocket

For schedules of opera and classical music concerts, see the local editions of the English-language publication *In Your Pocket*, www.inyourpocket.com, which contain good round-ups of nightlife in Warsaw, Kraków and Gdańsk, and *Warsaw Insider*, a free monthly publication for Warsaw.

Kraków's Słowacki Theatre

Theatre – National Opera (pl. Teatralny 1, tel: 022 692 0200, www.teatrwielki.pl) is the foremost venue in Poland for opera and ballet; Kiri Te Kanawa, Kathleen Battle and José Carreras have all sung here. For classical music concerts, the National Philharmonic Hall (ul. Jasna 5, tel: 022 551 7111, www.filharmonia.pl) and the intimate Opera Kameralna (al. Solidarności 76b, tel: 022 628 30 96, www.operakameralna.pl) are among the nation's best. There are also occasional concerts at the Royal Castle on pl. Zamkowy (tel: 022 355 5170). In Kraków, the Juliusz Słowacki Theatre (pl. Św. Ducha 1, tel: 012 424 4500, www.slowacki.krakow.pl) stages opera, as well as musicals, plays and concerts. Opera Krakowska (ul. Lubicz 48; tel: 012 296 6262; www.opera.krakow.pl) concentrates on productions of classical operas; while Kraków Filharmonia (ul. Zwierzyniecka 1; tel: 012 619 8721; www.filharmonia.krakow.pl) ranges beyond symphonies and hosts other orchestras, too. Concerts are also held at St Mary's Cathedral, SS Peter and Paul Church and on Wawel Hill in Kraków, and in summer at the Chopin Monument in Warsaw's Łazienki Park. In Gdańsk, the State Baltic Opera (Al. Zwycięstwa 15, tel: 058 763 4912/13, www.operabaltycka.pl) is one of the best in Poland, holding opera and symphonic concerts, while chamber music concerts are held at the Baltic

Philharmonic Hall (Ołowianka 1, tel: 058 320 6250, www.fil harmonia.gda.pl). In Poznań, opera is performed at the Teatr Wielki (ul. Fredry 9, tel: 061 659 0200, www.opera.poznan.pl) and classical music at Filharmonia Poznańska (ul. Św. Marcin 81, tel: 061 852 4708, www.filharmoniapoznanska.pl). Poznań is also well known for its acclaimed ballet company, the Polish Dance Theatre-Poznań Ballet (ul. Kozia 4, tel: 061 852 4242/41, www.ptt-poznan.pl).

Drama is staged almost entirely in Polish, tending to exclude most foreign tourists. Acting and directing are of a very high standard, though, and adventurous theatregoers who don't mind not understanding the language in order to see first-rate acting and production will find plenty of excellent performances, especially in Kraków, the epicentre of the Polish theatre world. The Stary Teatr, or Old Theatre (ul. Jagiellońska 1, tel: 012 422 8020, www.stary-teatr.pl) was Poland's first playhouse and is beautifully restored with a main stage and two ancillary stages. In Warsaw, top musicals of the Andrew Lloyd Webber variety land at Roma (ul. Nowogrodzka 49, tel: 022 628 8998, www.teatrroma.pl).

Cinema. Poland has an enviable cinematic tradition and has produced great film directors who've gone on to international success, including Krzysztof Kieślowski, Andrzej Wajda and Roman Polański. Poles are dedicated moviegoers, so in the cities you'll find plenty of subtitled Western films competing with homegrown products, showing at good, Dolby sound-equipped cinemas. Film admissions are cheap by comparison with many countries. Look out for the Warsaw Film Festival in October every year.

Clubs and bars. Poland's towns and cities teem with bars, pubs and clubs, and Poles are known as heavy drinkers, though today they drink more beer (piwo) than vodka and other spirits. You'll find Irish and English pubs and nightclubs across Poland.

Buddha Bar, Kraków

Bars in atmospheric cellars, and others above ground, have proliferated in recent years in Kraków's Old Town. With so many students in town, they're usually packed. There are so many it is difficult to single out only a few, but among the most interesting are: Prozak 2.0 (pl Dominikański 6); Art Club Błędne Koło (ul. Bracka 4); Stalowe Magnolie (ul. Św. Jana 15), which has live music and boudoir-style backrooms; Cień (next door at ul. Św. Jana 15); U Louisa (Rynek Główny 13); and, in Kazimierz, a nightlife hub where new places are opening all the time, Alchemia (ul. Estery 5) and Pub Propaganda (ul. Miodowa 20).

The distinction between cafés and bars is sometimes difficult to ascertain, but some of the many excellent cafés in Kraków include: Camelot (ul. Św. Tomasza 17), the historic Jama Michalika (ul. Floriańska 45) and Café Szzafé (ul. Felicjanek 10); while Singer (ul. Estery 20) is the quintessential Kazimierz café.

For jazz and blues clubs in Kraków, try Harris Piano Jazz Bar (Rynek Główny 28); U Muniaka (ul. Floriańska 3), Klub Indigo (ul. Floriańska 26) and Piec'Art (ul. Szewska 12).

Warsaw doesn't have quite as appealing a cluster of bars in one pub-crawl ready area, but the capital certainly has its share of watering holes and cafés. It has a mini collection of Irish pubs, including Jimmy Bradley's Irish Bar (ul. Sienna 39), Irish Pub (ul. Miodowa 3) and Cork Irish Pub (Al. Niepodległości 19). Other bars are Lolek (ul. Rokitnicka 20), the elegant Column Bar in the Hotel Bristol (ul. Krakowskie Przedmieście 42–44).

For cocktails try Paparazzi (ul. Mazowiecka 12). Nightclubs include Opera Club (pl. Teatralny 1), Platinum (ul. Fredry 6), and for jazz and blues Tygmont (ul. Mazowiecka 6-8). Gdańsk has a selection of lively pubs in its Main Town. The coolest are Café Kamienica (ul. Mariacka 37–39) and Flisak 76 (ul. Chlebnicka 9–10). For live jazz, check out the Elephant Club (Długi Targ 41–42) or for all kinds of music and more live happenings the studenty Klub Żak (ul. Grunwaldzka 195–197).

SPORTS

The most popular sport in Poland, as in most European nations, is football (soccer), although other sports including volleyball, handball, ice hockey, wind surfing and skiing are also popular. Being chosen as one of the host countries for Euro 2012 signalled Poland's arrival on the sporting world map. The countryside is ideal for outdoor enthusiasts, so

Tatra Mountains

Windsurfing in Puck Bay

visitors interested in horse-riding, skiing, fishing and hiking have myriad options.

Golf. If you're a golf enthusiast, head for the First Warsaw Golf and Country Club (ul. Golfowa, Rajszew, Jabłonna, tel: 022 782 4555, http://fwgcc.pl), an 18-hole course about 30km (19 miles) outside of the capital. Perhaps the best golfing is near the Baltic Sea, at the Postołowo Golf Club (Postołowo, tel: 058 683 7100, http://postolowo.com), 26km (16 miles) south of Gdańsk.

Hiking and walking. The vast countryside of Poland is ideal for leisurely walking and more athletic hiking. One of the best areas for both, especially for serious hikers, are the High Tatra Mountains around Zakopane.

Horse-riding. Equestrian holidays are becoming increasingly popular in Poland; many adventure travel operators offer them – look out for stables belonging to the Polish Equestrian Federation (Polski Związek Jeździecki). If you just want to get in the saddle for a short while, contact Patataj Horse-Riding School (Szkoła Jazdy Konnej, ul. Krótka 9, Kanie, tel: 022 758 5835; www.patataj.com) near Warsaw. There are a couple of dozen stables and riding schools in the environs of the capital (ask at the tourist information centre or your hotel for details).

Skiing. The best place for skiing is Zakopane, at the foot of the High Tatra Mountains in southeastern Poland. Skiing is

excellent, inexpensive and very popular with Poles and some
foreigners on ski packages, even though facilities lag behind
resorts in the Alps and Pyrenees.

Swimming and water sports. In Warsaw, the Victoria, Marriott
and Bristol hotels have swimming pools. Less ritzy are these
pools: Aquapark Wesolandia (ul. Wspólna 4, tel: 022 773 9191,
www.wesolandia.pl), Polna (ul. Polna 7a, tel: 022 825 71 34,
www.osir-polna.pl) and Wodny Park (ul. Merliniego 4, tel: 022
854 0130, www.wodnypark.com.pl). Kraków also has several
pools open to visitors: Park Wodny (ul. Dobrego Pasterza 126,
tel: 012 616 3190, www.parkwodny.pl) is the best year-round,
though open-air pools are available in summer. There are
also hotel pools at the Copernicus (ul. Kanonicza 16), its sister
hotel the Stary (ul. Szczepańska 5) and at the Novotel Kraków
Centrum (ul. Kosciuszki 5) and the Sheraton (ul. Powiśle 7).

The most popular areas for boating and other water
sports are the Mazurian Lakes district in northeastern
Poland and near the towns along the Bay of Gdańsk, on the
Baltic Sea.

Football. Football (soccer) is Poland's most popular spectator
sport. Warsaw's first-division football team is Legia Warszawa
(ul. Łazienkowska 3, tel: 022 628 4303, www.legia.com).

CHILDREN

Travelling with children in Poland is a matter of being flexible,
creative, and putting together activities to keep the kids interested when palaces, castles and rebuilt old towns impress
them less than they do their parents. Many of the activities
listed below are in the capital, Warsaw, where there is simply
a greater abundance of facilities.

Warsaw Zoo (ul. Ratuszowa 1–3, tel: 022 619 4041, www.
zoo.waw.pl) has been open since 1928. The habitats of some
4,000 animals, including Siberian tigers, kangaroos, cheetahs,

Fountain in the Old Town, Wrocław

crocodiles, snow leopards and an unusual red panda, are spread across 40 hectares (99 acres). The zoo also has a free-flight bird hall.

Another option for kids in Warsaw is the Teatr Guliwer (ul. Różana 16, tel: 022 845 1677, www.teatrguliwer. waw.pl).

For children with energy to burn, there are water parks and swimming pools in summer, and ice rinks in winter. To go ice skating in Warsaw, check out the Stegny (ul. Inspektowa 1, tel: 022 842 3872, http://aktywnawarszawa.waw.pl/stegny) or Towarzystwo Łyżwiarstwa Figurowego Walley (ul. Kombatantów 60, Julianów, tel: 0515 184 555, www.walley.pl). During winter there is also an ice rink at the National Stadium (www.pgenarodowy.pl). Another fast-paced sport is go-karts. In Warsaw, race the kids over to Pole Position (ul. Graniczna 15, tel: 0606 339 338, or ul. Powstańców Śląskich 126; tel: 0512 597 587, www.pole-position.pl). If your kids like bowling, you'll find facilities in all the major cities. In the Malta lake district of Poznań, there are many facilities ideal for children, including a man-made ski slope and an exhilarating toboggan run.

For older kids who enjoy hiking and skiing, the area around Zakopane in the Tatra Mountains is the best in Poland. Sure to be popular with kids are the 700-year-old Wieliczka Salt Mines near Kraków (see page 57), where you first descend 378 steps, then continue through long corridors and see chapels and figures (including the Seven Dwarves) entirely carved out of salt, and finally zoom up to ground level via a fast and slightly shaky bare-bones elevator.

FESTIVALS AND EVENTS

January Opera Rara festival, Kraków

February Sea Shanty Festival (www.shanties.krakow.pl), Kraków

March/April Holy Week religious celebrations, all Poland; Misteria Paschalia organ music festival (www.misteriapaschalia.com), Kraków; Beethoven Easter Festival (www.beethoven.org.pl), Warsaw

March Music Festival (www.wiosnamuzyczna.pl), Poznań

April OffPlusCamera (www.offcamera.pl) independent film festival, Kraków; Festival of Science and Art (/www.festiwal.torun.pl), Toruń; Jazz on the Odra (http://jazznadodra.pl), Wrocław

May International Street Art Festival (http://sztukaulicy.pl), Warsaw; ProBaltica Music and Art Festival (www.probaltica.art.pl), Toruń; Film Music Festival (http://fmf.fm), Kraków; Night of the Museums, countrywide; Good Beer Festival (www.festiwaldobregopiwa.pl), Wrocław

June Old Town Summer Jazz Days (www.jazznastarowce.pl), Warsaw; Folk Art Festival, Zamość; Dragon Parade, Kraków; National Festival of Polish Song, Opole; Burn Selector Electronic and Dance Music Festival, Kraków; Midsummer's Night Wianki celebrations, Kraków

24 June St John's Feast Day, especially in Warsaw, Kraków and Poznań

June/July Festival of Jewish Culture (www.jewishfestival.pl), Kraków; Opener Music Festival (http://opener.pl), Gdańsk

July/August Dominican Fair (http://jarmarkdominika.pl), Gdańsk; Nowe Horyzonty Film Festival (www.nowehoryzonty.pl), Wrocław

August International Song Festival, Sopot; Carillon Festival (www.carillon.pl), Gdansk; International Festival of Highland Folklore (http://festiwale.zakopane.pl), Zakopane; Artus Jazz Festival, Toruń; Transatlantyk Film and Music Festival (http://transatlantyk.org), Łódź

September Sacrum Profanum (http://sacrumprofanum.com), Kraków "Singer's Warsaw" Jewish Culture Festival, Warsaw

October Warsaw Film Festival (www.wff.pl)

November Explorers' Festival (www.explorersfestival.pl), Łódz; 11 November Independence Day (countrywide); St Martin's Festival, Poznań

December Nativity Crib competition, Kraków (Rynek); New Year's Eve Wow open-air club night Kraków (Rynek)

EATING OUT

Polish cuisine ranges from light and elegant to rich and hearty, invariably served in generous portions. Soups are a speciality, while potatoes and dumplings are a staple, and vegetables are available in a variety of dishes. Given its shifting borders over the centuries, it's not surprising that Polish cooking also shows the influence of several national cuisines, namely of its Ukrainian, German, Lithuanian and Russian neighbours.

Many people in other countries are familiar with common Polish dishes, such as *pierogi* (stuffed dumplings), *barszcz* (beetroot soup) and *kiełbasa* (Polish sausage), as well as menu favourites such as herrings, charcuterie or sauerkraut.

The restaurant scene in Poland, like almost everything else, has changed dramatically in the years since the fall of the Communist regime. Opportunities for eating out, at least

Street vendors cooking up Polish sausage

as far as fine dining was concerned, used to be rare, and shortages and rationing were common. This is no longer the case. Restaurants of all styles have blossomed in all the big towns, though traditional restaurants serving classic Polish cuisine have not disappeared, thankfully. They should be the focus of any visitor's dining habits in Poland.

Book ahead wherever possible at top-tier restaurants in Kraków and Warsaw. Many restaurants remain open throughout the afternoon, and most stay open late, until 11pm or midnight.

WHERE TO EAT

Visitors will mostly eat their meals in a *restauracja* (restaurant). These range from inexpensive eateries, where office workers take their lunch, to upmarket dining rooms frequented far more by foreign visitors and a small handful of elite Poles than by ordinary citizens; restaurants have table service.

A café *(kawiarnia)* is not strictly a coffeehouse. Most also have a menu and serve everything from snacks to full meals at all hours of the day. Another traditional eatery is the cheap, cafeteria-style, self-service creature called a bar *mleczny*, literally a milk bar. Often you can get a good, home-cooked and filling plate in one of these places for very little.

WHEN TO EAT

In Poland breakfast *(śniadanie)* is generally served between the hours of 7am and 10am. Poles typically eat bread or a roll served with butter, cheese, and ham or sausage. Eggs for breakfast are not uncommon. At most upmarket hotels, a basic international breakfast buffet will generally be served. Often you will find local pastries and possibly some foods you may not think of as usual breakfast fare.

The nation's favourite - pierogi

Lunch *(obiad)*, generally served between 1pm and 4pm, is traditionally the main meal of the day, a fact reflected in the quantities in which it is served. Lunch typically consists of three courses: soup, main course and dessert.

Dinner *(kolacja)* is served from early evening onwards, and it can be similar to and nearly as substantial as the *obiad* or considerably lighter, with a similar selection to what would be served for breakfast.

POLISH COOKING

Certain ingredients are essential to traditional Polish cuisine: fish, game, potatoes, wild mushrooms and other vegetables. One of the most distinctive flavours of Polish cooking is sourness, but dishes can also be spicy hot or sweet.

Some traditional dishes are cooked in lard, although oil or butter is more likely to be the norm these days. If portions are too hefty for you, order soup and then an appetiser instead of a main, and try to leave room for dessert.

The undisputed frontrunner of Polish folk dishes is the ubiquitous *pierogi*, which are originally from Russia and date back to medieval times. *Pierogi* can be sweet or savoury. Ravioli-like dumplings are filled with one of a variety of stuffings, including fresh cabbage or sauerkraut mixed with mushrooms; cheese and potatoes; or soft fruits in summer. Small *pierogi* are sometimes served in soups. Stuffed cabbage, called *gołąbki* or little pigeons, is another traditional dish. The leaves are filled with minced meat and rice, and usually served with tomato or mushroom sauce. Poles are also very fond of potato pancakes and potato dumplings.

On restaurant menus, note that main courses do not usually include accompaniments. Potatoes, salads and other side dishes are listed under *dodatki* and cost extra.

SOUP

Soup *(zupa)* is immensely popular with locals and always on the menu. Most Poles think a meal incomplete without soup (some visitors may find Polish soups, on the other hand, to be complete meals). *Barszcz czerwony* (red beetroot soup) is an ancient recipe; the authentic version has a distinctive taste. It can be served clear or with cream and with small ravioli-like dumplings. Beetroot soup made with vegetable stock and served with mushroom-filled *uszki* (small ravioli) is traditional for Christmas Eve. *Żurek*, or white *barszcz*, is made from rye flour then fermented, before being seasoned. It is

Oscypek, a smoked cheese, is a Zakopane speciality

sometimes served with sausage or a hardboiled egg. *Chłodnik* is a cold summer beetroot soup which includes thick soured cream combined with cucumbers, radishes, chives and dill. *Ogórkowa* (dill cucumber soup) is also sour, as is *kapuśniak* (sauerkraut soup). Other soups to enjoy are *grzybowa* (mushroom soup), *szczawiowa*, or sorrel soup, and *zupa koperkowa*, which features the national herb, dill.

STARTERS

The classic starter *(przekąski)* is herring, which can be served in olive oil, or with soured cream, or pickled with lots of chopped onions. Poland also produces a wide range of sausages and hams, which are a speciality and a national favourite of Poles. You'll also find jellied carp, pike and smoked eel as appetisers, as well as smaller portions of favourite main courses, such as *pierogi* or potato pancakes.

Smalec – goes great with a local beer

MAIN COURSES

Meat *(mięso; dania mięsne)*. Poland is a nation of avid carnivores, and to most Poles, a meal of substance includes meat. Pork is by far the most popular meat dish. The classic preparation is a pork cutlet prepared with fried onions, coated in breadcrumbs and served with stewed cabbage. Roast pork is eaten both hot and cold. Hot pot roast may be served with dried prunes. Beef is less common, though *zrazy zawijane* (beef rolls filled with bacon, dark bread and mushrooms) is a standard dish. *Flaki po polsku* (tripe stew) is thin strips of beef tripe, boiled in meat and vegetable stock and served with dark bread.

> ### Classic dish
>
> The meat dish not to be missed in Poland is *bigos*, a classic hunter's stew and the supreme Polish winter meal. It consists of fresh white cabbage and sauerkraut, usually cooked with different types of meat, game and sausage (meat and cabbage in equal proportion).

Game *(dziczyzna)* and poultry *(drób)*. Game is very popular, as you might expect from the national affinity for meat and rich tastes. Venison *(sarna)* is usually reserved for elite restaurants, as are wild boar *(dzik)* and other 'exotic' game. Look, too, for hare *(zając)* and pheasant *(bażant)*. Chicken *(kurczak)* is popular and is typically stuffed and roasted. Chicken soup is another great Polish favourite, as is roasted duck *(kaczka)* with apples.

Fish *(dania rybne)*. Fish is as popular on menus as pork and other meats, with pike, eel, perch, sturgeon and others – boiled, fried or roasted – found in most good restaurants. Carp is a particular favourite (especially on Christmas Eve), often served in aspic or Polish sauce with raisins and almonds.

Vegetarian dishes *(potrawy jarskie* or *wegetariańskie)*. Vegetarian restaurants are now much less of a rarity in Poland, especially in bigger cities. Although classic milk bars began basically as vegetarian places, most have now added a few meat dishes and these old-fashioned eateries may follow the Communist-era habit of 'improving' vegetables by using lard when frying. In most restaurants, vegetable accompaniments have to be ordered separately and can be very creative.

Vegetarians should steer towards potato pancakes or dumplings stuffed with fruit, *pierogi* filled with cheese and potato, and crepes. Salads include tomato salads, sliced cucumbers in sour cream, and sauerkraut.

DESSERTS

Poles are great eaters of pastries and sweets. Among those you're likely to find are *eklerki* (éclairs), *napoleonki* (millefeuille), *sernik* (cheesecake), *szarlotka* (apple cake), *makowiec* (poppy-seed roll) and *mazurek* – thin flat cakes topped with nuts and fruits.

DRINKS

Poland has begun to make wine from grapes but production is still in its infancy. However, wine is becoming more and more popular, and you will find imported wines are available in cafés and restaurants. In any good restaurant you'll probably find a range of French, Italian and Spanish wines alongside

THE NATIONAL SPIRIT

The Poles and Russians may bicker about who created it, but vodka *(wódka)* is a staple of the Polish diet. Most vodkas are distilled from rye, but a few are made from potatoes – both types have a distinct character. It is usually clear, though you'll also find coloured and flavoured versions. Wyborowa (distilled from rye) is one of the best popular brands, with a range of flavoured vodkas; look also for Luksusowa (distilled from potatoes) and Żubrówka (which is flavoured with bison grass from the Bialowieża forest), and kosher vodkas.

Vodka is heavily ritualised. If you visit someone at home, it's polite to take a bottle, though you're not expected to empty it.

those from the New World. Prices may be steeper than you might expect.

Polish beers, or *piwo*, go well with heavy, spicy foods; except at the most formal of restaurants, it is as acceptable to drink beer with a meal as it is wine. Polish beers have improved a lot recently, although they do not enjoy the same reputation as their Czech and German counterparts. In summer, cafés may serve beer flavoured with fruit or ginger syrup, while mulled beer is as popular as mulled wine in winter. Among the best-known brands are Żywiec, EB, Warka and Tyskie.

Vodka, the national spirit, usually taken neat

The new craze are the microbreweries sprouting across the country and offering craft beers including wheat beers, ales stouts and many others. For information on brewery tours and the Brewing Museum at the Tyskie Brewery in Tychy, 20km (12 miles) south of Katowice, see www.kp.pl.

Coffee *(kawa)* is usually served black (unless you ask for milk) or with just a dash of milk. Espresso and capuccino are widely available. Tea *(herbata)*, usually served with lemon, is drunk by most Poles.

International soft drinks are readily available. Though tap water in cities is safe to drink, its taste can leave a lot to be desired, hence mineral water *(woda mineralna)* is popular with Poles.

MENU READER

barszcz beetroot soup	**mięso** meat
befsztyk beef steak	**ogórek** cucumber
bigos sauerkraut and meat dish	**piwo** beer
	polędwica sirloin steak
chleb bread	**ryba** fish
frytki chips/fries	**ryż** rice
gołąbki stuffed cabbage leaves	**sałatka** salad
	ser cheese
golonka boiled pork knuckle	**szynka** ham
grzyb mushroom	**woda** water
herbata tea	**wódka** vodka
jarzyny vegetables	**ziemniaki** potatoes
kawa coffee	**zrazy** stuffed beef rolls
kotlet fried pork cutlet	**zupa** soup
kurczak chicken	**żurek** rye-flour soup

Enjoying a meal in Kraków

PLACES TO EAT

All the restaurants below accept major credit cards except where noted. The following guidelines denote an average three-course meal for one, excluding wine and service:

$$$$** over 200zł   **$$$ 100–200zł
$$** 50–100zł   **$ below 50zł

KRAKOW

Café Ariel $$ *ul. Szeroka 18, tel: 012 421 7920;* http://ariel-krakow. pl. Open daily for breakfast, lunch and dinner. In the heart of Kazimierz, the Jewish quarter, is this charming long-established Jewish (but non-kosher) restaurant. Nightly (8pm) performances by a klezmer music trio. Great fun.

Camelot Café $$ *ul. Św. Tomasza 17, tel: 012 421 0123;* www.came lot.pl. Open daily for breakfast, lunch and dinner. Fashionable and funky café popular with the university crowd – a good place to sip tea, have a beer or enjoy a light meal. Excellent salads, soups, sandwiches and desserts. Medieval cellar vibe at street level.

Chimera Salad Bar $ *ul. Św. Anny 3, tel: 012 292 1212;* http://chimera. com.pl. A series of underground vaulted rooms, open 9am–10pm, offering inexpensive self-service salads and snacks. There is also a street-level garden for summer. Extremely popular so you may have to queue, particularly at lunchtimes. Do not confuse it with its equally excellent sibling restaurant, a few doors down, which specialises in high-class Polish traditional cooking and game in season at suitably higher prices.

Chłopskie Jadło $$–$$$ *ul. Św. Jana 3, tel: 0725 100 535;* www. chlopskiejadlo.pl. Open daily for lunch and dinner. The name means 'Peasant Kitchen', an apt description of this excellent chain of rustic Polish restaurants. Fun, colourful, farmhouse décor and classic, robust foods, including soups, *pierogi*, fish and meat dishes, with half-litre beers, lard to spread on your bread and accompanied by folk music – as if in the Polish countryside.

Cyrano de Bergerac $$$$ *ul. Sławkowska 26, tel: 012 411 7288;* www.cyranodebergerac.pl. Open daily for lunch and dinner. An elegant cellar restaurant serving French food at French prices to the city's elite plus passing celebrities. A veritable institution if, of course, you can afford it.

Da Pietro $$ *Rynek Główny 17, tel: 012 422 3279;* www.dapietro.pl. Open daily for lunch and dinner. Right on the Market Square, in a delightful cellar, this is a good place to get an Italian fix without breaking the bank. Large portions and a good list of pastas.

Milkbar Tomasza $$ *ul. Św. Tomasza 24, tel: 012 422 17 06.* Open daily for breakfast, lunch and dinner. The stylish eatery located on one of the most picturesque Kraków streets is a mix of traditional Polish *bar mleczny* ('milk bar') and American diner. The food is simple: *pierogi* (dumplings), pancakes, salads, sandwiches.

Momo $ *ul. Dietla 49, tel: 0609 685 775.* Open daily for lunch and dinner. Wholesome, vegetarian food in a small and very informal restaurant between the Old Town and Kazimierz. One of the few places in the country to serve brown rice.

Padre $$ *ul. Wiślna 11, tel: 012 430 6299;* http://restauracja-padre.pl. Open daily for lunch and dinner. A real gem of a restaurant tucked away in an old church cellar; the menu features a beguiling mix of decent Indian and Italian food. Good music policy too.

Pod Aniołami $$$ *ul. Grodzka 35, tel: 012 421 3999;* www.podaniolami.pl. Open daily for lunch and dinner. A cool and elegant medieval-looking cellar with stone walls, wood tables and rugs on the walls. There's also a breezy interior courtyard for outdoor dining in summer. Specialises in local cuisine, including all kinds of grilled meat dishes.

Szara $$$ *Rynek Główny 6, tel: 012 421 6669;* http://szara.pl. Open daily for lunch and dinner. Elegant brasserie-style setting in an historic market square building, with an adventurous range of European dishes to enjoy.

U Romana $ *ul. Kanonicza Św. Tomasza 1543 (6th floor), tel: 012 423 20 81 ext.,* http://uromana.com.pl. Open Mon–Fri for lunch and dinner,

Sat lunch only. Cheap cafeteria located in the seat of the Kraków Music Academy. The food is simple and traditional, but the most important is the wonderful panoramic view over the roofs of the city.

Wierzynek $$$$ *Rynek Główny 15, tel: 012 424 9600;* http://wierzynek.pl. Open daily for lunch and dinner. Kraków's most famous restaurant claims to have served its first banquet in 1364. It has a modern approach to traditional Polish cuisine and the menu, which includes lots of game, is served among antiques and historic treasures in grand rooms that have welcomed many presidents and stars.

ZAKOPANE

Bąkowo Zohylina $$ *ul. Piłsudskiego 6, tel: 018 206 6216.* Open daily for lunch and dinner. This excellent highlander restaurant would be 'big fun', as my Polish friend likes to say, even if the food weren't terrific (which it is). The rustic décor – a wooden lodge with fur pelts and stuffed animals – is the perfect backdrop for dishes like sour cabbage soup and heavy portions of meat. A regionally costumed band plays mountain music with great showmanship.

Gubałówka $$ *ul. Gubałówka 2, tel: 018 206 3630.* Open daily for lunch and dinner. Typical *góral* food served inside a large wooden lodge, or outdoors on the terrace in good weather, at the top of Zakopane's funicular train ride. What the place lacks in sophistication it more than compensates for with its stunning views of the mountains.

Gazdówka $$ *ul. Jagiellońska 18, tel: 018 206 43 27,* www.restauracja-gazdowka.pl. Open daily for lunch and dinner. Situated in a beautiful wooden villa built at the beginning of the 20th century. The menu served in this rustic and spacious interior is a mix of traditional cuisine from Podhale with some modern flavours.

ZAMOSC

Bohema $$ *ul. S.Staszica 29, tel: 084 638 1414,* www.bohema zamosc.pl. Open daily for lunch and dinner. One street away from the marketplace, this restaurant in an air-conditioned vaulted basement, also has a garden for summer lunches. The menu ranges over European and Polish dishes making it a good choice whether you want a snack or a more substantial meal.

Padwa $$–$$$ *ul. Staszica 23 (Rynek), tel: 084 638 6256*, www. padwa.pl. Open daily for lunch and dinner. A cellar restaurant off the Market Square, it's like a dimly lit dungeon, with massive columns and arches and a vaulted ceiling. Though it has a vaguely pre-glasnost feel to it, with its glitzy 'drink bar' at one end, you can't go wrong with Padwa's upstanding Polish fare, such as *pierogi* and soups.

WARSAW

Adler $$ *ul. Mokotowska 69, tel: 022 628 7384*, www.adlerrestauracja. pl. Open daily for lunch and dinner. This cosy, popular German restaurant revels in Wiener Schnitzel, sausages and German beers. Expect large portions and an occasionally noisy clientele (perhaps something to do with all that beer...).

Atelier Amaro $$$$ *ul. Afrykola 1, tel: 022 628 57 47*, www.atelier amaro.pl. Open Tue–Fri for lunch and Mon-Sat for dinner. Easily Warsaw's best restaurant and the first Michelin star in Poland. The chef Modest Amaro creates innovative Polish cuisine from the freshest ingredients and sometimes forgotten traditional Polish products. Advance booking essential.

Butchery & Wine $$$$ *ul. Żurawia 22, tel: 022 502 31 18*, www. butcheryandwine.pl. Open Mon-Sat for lunch and dinner. This airy, simple and understatedly smart restaurant serves arguably the best steaks in Warsaw. You can even sample Polish wine from the Lubuskie region. It's pricey, but you won't regret it.

Czerwony Wieprz $$$ *ul. Żelazna 68 7, tel: 022 850 31 44*, www. czerwonywieprz.pl. Open daily for lunch and dinner. A theme restaurant, Red Pig tries to recreate the atmosphere of Communist Poland. Besides the extravagant decor and names of the dishes, it's a really good example of traditional Polish cooking popular 50 years ago.

Dyspensa $$$ *ul. Mokotowska 39, tel: 022 629 9989,* www.dyspensa. pl. Open daily for lunch and dinner. An absolutely terrific-looking place decked out to look like a welcoming country kitchen. Very popular and atmospheric at night, when locals and a good many expats pack it to enjoy international dishes including duck *à l'orange*.

Kuźnia Smaku $$$ *ul. Mazowiecka 10, tel: 022 826 3024;* www. kuzniasmaku.pl. Open daily for breakfast, lunch and dinner Popular place with a pre-war ambiance, concentrating on authentic Polish and Russian dishes, such as roast sturgeon with wild mushrooms.

Le Cedre $$$ *al. Solidarności 61 and 84, tel: 022 670 1166,* www. lecedre.pl. Open daily for lunch and dinner. Like a scene out of *Lawrence of Arabia*, this immensely popular Lebanese restaurant (there are two branches in the same street) titillates the taste buds with a menu of spicy meat dishes served with lashings of hot flat bread and of course the obligatory bubble pipe for dessert. Belly dancing entertainment is sometimes provided.

Marconi $$$$ *ul. Krakowskie Przedmieście 42–44, tel: 022 551 1000,* www.restauracjamarconi.pl. Open daily for lunch and dinner. As you might expect from the opulent Bristol Hotel, this is a refined, traditional restaurant serving excellent Polish and Italian cuisine. One of the city's most luxurious and sophisticated dining rooms.

Opasły Tom $$$ *ul. Foksal 17, tel: 022 621 18 81,* www.kregliccy. pl. Open daily for lunch and dinner. Situated in a former bookstore of the famous Polisih editorial PWN is a small place with a real *cuisine d´auteur* by chef Agata Wojda. The menu is short and seasonal and all the ingredients are fresh. You can sample some Polish wines.

Różana $$$ *Chocimska 7, tel: 022 848 1225,* www.restauracja rozana.com.pl. Beautifully decorated in an antique style, this townhouse restaurant set in a romantic garden with splashing fountains, has a wonderful selection of Polish dishes.

Zielony Niedźwiedź $$$ *ul. Smolna 4, tel: 0 795 794 784,* www. kafezn.pl. Open Tue–Sun for lunch and dinner, Mon only dinner.

The menu is seasonal and features a modern interpretation of Polish cuisine, with some international influences. Besides some national staples such as goose or local fish, there are always some vegetarian options. Delicacies such as Polish honey, jellies, cheeses or excellent yoghurts which are available on shelves near the bar can be bought for home. Equally amazing is the wine list with bottles bought directly from the best wineries.

GDANSK

Bar Pod Rybą $ *ul. Piwna 61-63 , tel: 058 305 1307,* http://barpod ryba.pl. Open daily for breakfast, lunch and dinner. This magnificent little restaurant serves jacket potatoes to eat either in or as a takeaway and fried fish. Superb value and a visual treat, portions are both delicious and enormous. It gets busy during the week, but the wait is more than worth the effort. There's a summer garden for smokers, while inside the paintings of Old Gdańsk by the owner are for sale. Highly recommended.

Metamorfoza $$-$$$$ *ul. Szeroka 22/23 – 24/26, tel: 058 320 30 30,* www.restauracjametamorfoza.pl. Open daily for lunch and dinner. This gourmet restaurant offers a real culinary adventure. The cuisine is a creative interpretation of Polish and international cooking.

Restauracja Baryłka $$ *ul. Długie Pobrzeże 24, tel: 058 301 4938,* www.barylka.pl. The name means 'little barrel' and your stomach might resemble that after a traditional Polish meal here of duck with apple stuffing or one of the other dishes from the regional menu. Though there are some international dishes, too, even the salads look pretty filling. The setting is suitably traditional – near the river in an ancient part of the city.

Pod Łososiem $$$$ *ul. Szeroka 52–4, tel: 058 301 7652,* http://podlososiem.com.pl. Open daily for lunch and dinner. Acclaimed as Gdańsk's finest formal restaurant, 'Under the Salmon' is a beautifully ornate establishment that used to be the distillery of Goldwasser vodka, which is infused with flecks of 23-carat gold. Posh and plush, with a sophisticated international menu, this is *the* place in Gdańsk for a special night out.

Targ Rybny $$$$ *ul. Targ Rybny 6C, tel: 058 320 9011*, www.targ rybny.pl. Open daily for lunch and dinner. Next to the fishmarket that dates back to 1343, this restaurant serves Kashubian dishes take their cue from the Kashubian fishwives who traded in this part of town, and the menu features monthly seasonal specials.

SOPOT

Bulaj $$$ *al. Mamuszki 22, tel: 058 551 5129*, www.bulaj.pl. Open daily for lunch and dinner. Almost on the beach, this restaurant subscribes to the 'slow food' philosophy but its ambitions are hardly laidback. If you want a change from fish, there are wild boar dumplings and stewed rabbit with chickpeas on the menu.

TORUN

Karczma Spichrz $$ *ul. Mostowa 1, tel: 056 657 1140*, www.spichrz. pl. Open daily for lunch and dinner. Converted from a granary in the old town and bedecked with wooden beams, this hotel restaurant serves familiar local dishes such as you might get in a traditional Polish inn, to the accompaniment of live folk music.

Petite Fleur $$ *ul. Piekary 25, tel: 056 621 5100*, www.petitefleur.pl. Open daily for lunch and dinner. Serving sophisticated French and Polish cuisine, Toruń's most elegant restaurant is in the brick-walled cellar of a boutique hotel in the Old Town with heavy ceiling beams, romantic lighting and excellent service.

Pierogarnia Stary Młyn $-$$ *ul. Żeglarska Łazienna 28, tel: 056 621 03 09*, www.pierogarnie.com. Open daily for lunch and dinner. It's a chain, but each branch is offers regional versions of traditional Polish *pierogi* (dumplings).The portions are big and tasty.

ŁÓDŹ

Bistro Tari Bari $$-$$$ *ul. Piotrkowska 138/140, tel: 042 728 50 73* http://offpiotrkowska.com. Open daily for lunch and dinner. Airy, unpretentious, modern bistro located in an old factory. Good Italian menu that changes daily; the *pannacotta* is amazing. Gets crowded.

POZNAN

Gospoda Młyńskie Koło $$$ *ul. Browarna 37, tel: 061 878 9935,* http://mlynskiekolo.pl. Open daily for lunch and dinner. In an old water mill just five minutes from the Market Square, this folksy restaurant serves Polish grilled specialities including boar and duck stuffed with apples. Great desserts and a lovely fireplace.

Jadalnia $$ *ul. Grunwaldzka 182, tel: 061 883 031 313,* www.jada lnia.com. Open daily for lunch and dinner. Spacious modern interior, funny lampshades, long tables with different style chairs. The simple and tasty dishes changes every day, menu online.

Ratuszova $$$ *Stary Rynek 55, tel: 061 858 0513,* www.ratuszova. pl. Open daily for lunch and dinner. Wonderfully atmospheric candlelit cellar restaurant on the Old Market Square. Decorated with theatre costumes. Hearty, rustic cooking with cheery service.

WROCŁAW

Steinhaus Café & Restuarant $$$ *Włodkowica 11, tel: 0512 931 071,* www.steinhaus.pl. Open daily from 11. Smart interior with a modern feel: wooden floors, black chalkboard, low lighting. Come for Jewish, Polish and Lviv specialities. There's no pork on the menu but duck, turkey, beef and fish reign supreme. Try the goose with red cabbage and dumplings - delicious. Great wine list.

Central Café $-$$ *Ul Św Antoniego 10, tel: 071 794 96 23,* http:// centralcafe.pl. Open: Mon–Sat 9am–9pm, Sun 9am–4pm. This popular, always busy place in central Wrocław is good for a quick lunch or breakfast. It offers the biggest selection of bagels in Poland. The cakes are also fresh and tasty; cheesecake and carrot cake are especially recommended.

A–Z TRAVEL TIPS

A Summary of Practical Information

A

ACCOMMODATION

Accommodation for visitors to Poland has improved greatly in recent years, with hotels offering modern facilities, often in beautiful old buildings. However, especially at the mid- to lower-range, choices can be limited. Hotels in Poland are unofficially graded from one to five stars, and those rating three to five are of comparable international standard. Warsaw, Kraków and other larger cities have an increasing number of top-flight, five-star hotels targeting business travellers and upmarket tourists. Several familiar international hotel brand names can be found, although home-grown independent enterprises are often more characterful.

If all the higher grade hotels are full, or beyond your budget, the best option can be to stay slightly out of town in a pension or guest-house hotel. Other options are accommodation in private homes or a self-catering apartment. There are also more than 200 registered campsites and a network of youth hostels in the major cities. Hostels can be an excellent choice for anyone wanting simple accommodation, as some are centrally situated, eg, in Kraków, and offer one or two private rooms as well as the more usual shared accommodation in larger dormitory rooms.

It is essential to book ahead during peak season (May to October). Tourism Information Offices (including those at airports) will provide lists of accommodation.

Do you have a room? **Czy są wolne pokoje?**
How much is it? **Ile kosztuje?**
single **pojedynczy pokój**
double **podwójny pokój**
without bath/with bath **bez łazienki/z łazienką**
expensive **drogi**

Room prices, which should be posted at the reception desk, usually include VAT and often but not always include breakfast. Outside of the most expensive hotels, prices are generally lower than those in other European countries. Confusingly, hotels may list their prices in US dollars, euros or Polish złoty, though payment is always in złoty.

AIRPORTS *(lotnisko)*

Warsaw: International flights arrive and depart from the very modern and recently extended Warsaw Chopin Airport (ul. Żwirki i Wigury 1; www.lotnisko-chopina.pl), formerly known as Okęcie Airport, southwest of the capital. There are car-hire agencies, left luggage facilities, money exchange desks, cash machines, travel agents, a restaurant and a tourist information office as well as hotels. It takes about 30 minutes to get from the airport to the centre of Warsaw. A taxi should cost no more than 40 zł (at night) depending on which one you choose. Some of the taxis waiting out front may look official, but are not and will charge exorbitant prices, so be careful. Avoid taxi drivers offering their services inside the terminal.

If you need to take a taxi, call for one at the information desk: Ele Sky Taxi (tel: 022 811 1111), Sawa Taxi (tel: 022 644 4444) or Super Taxi (tel: 022 196-22/196-61). Three buses run daily from 5am–11pm from the airport (watch out for pickpockets). The 175 stops at the Dworzec Centralny main train station, while the 148 goes to Praga, and the 188 passes Metro Politechnika in the city centre. Bus 331 (Mon–Fri until 6pm) passes Metro Wilanowska and the N32 night bus gets you to the Dw. Centralny train station when the other buses have finished for the night.

Trains operated by the Szybka Kolej Miejska (Fast Urban Railway or SKM; www.skm.warszawa.pl) and Koleje Mazowieckie (Mazovian Railways) leave every 15 minutes from the underground station adjacent to the airport terminal. Line S2 goes to Warszawa Śródmieście (in the centre of the city) while S3 to the Warszawa Wschodnia railway terminal across the Vistula river. Koleje Mazowieckie offer connections to Modlin airport (a shuttle bus operates between the terminal and the railway station).

Modlin airport (WMI; ul. Gen. Wiktora Thommee 1a, Nowy Dwór Mazowiecki; tel: 022 346 4000; www.modlinairport.pl) is situated about 40 km north of Warsaw. It's a relatively new modern hub for low-cost carriers including Ryanair and Wizzair. Koleje Mazowieckie (www.mazowieckie.com.pl) and Modlin shuttle bus (www.modlin bus.pl) operate regular services between the city centre and the airport. Check their respective websites for details.

Kraków: John Paul II International Airport (KRK; Balice, ul. Kapitana Medweckiego 1, Balice; tel: 801 055 000; www.krakowairport. pl), is 18km west of town. The fastest way to get there is by the Koleje Małopolskie (http://malopolskiekoleje.pl) train which runs from the city's central train station every half an hour between 4am–11.30pm. The journey takes only 17 minutes. Alternatively, buses 292, 902 and 208 take slower roundabout routes through the suburbs to the Old Town and the train station. Tickets can be bought from the driver (you need to have the exact change) and vending machines. An official Kraków Airport Taxi service (www.krk taxi.pl) offers fixed-rate services based on distance covered.

Gdańsk: With flights arriving from all over Europe, Gdańsk Lech Wałęsa Airport (GDN; ul Slowackiego 200, Rębiechowo; tel: 048 525 673 531; www.airport.gdansk.pl) is the third most important airport in the country, and serves not only the Tri-city area but travellers from Toruń and Szczecin, too. Fast growing in popularity, it is about 10km (6 miles) and 20 minutes' drive west of the city centre. A new terminal is linked with the city centre by the PKM trains that run about every 15 minutes, mostly to Gdańsk-Wrzeszcz station (some continue to the city's main station or even to Gdynia). The railway station is just outside the terminal and can be reached through the footbridge. Tickets are available from SKM, ZKM vending machines and on the train (cash only). Public buses operating to/from the airport include no. 110 to Gdańsk-Wrzeszcz railway station, no. 210

& N3 (nightbus) to Gdańsk Główny – the city's main railway station – and no.122 that runs to Sopot. The Neptun Taxi rank (tel: 196 86) is outside the main terminal entrance. The journey should cost about 50zł to 70zł, but make sure you agree a price before setting off.

B

BUDGETING FOR YOUR TRIP

Though prices have risen in the past few years, mainly because of the złoty's relative strength against other currencies, Poland remains one of the most inexpensive European countries to visit for tourists from Western Europe and North America. Still, visitors expecting the dirt-cheap Central Europe of the recent past may be in for a bit of a surprise. Four- and five-star hotels in Warsaw and Kraków are now nearly as costly as those in Western Europe. However, many facets of daily life remain true bargains for visitors: the highly efficient public transport system, restaurants and cafés, and museums and concert performances.

Transport to Poland. For most Europeans, Warsaw or Kraków is a short, fairly inexpensive flight or train ride away. The fast-changing market for air travel with rising taxes and fuel surcharges makes it more important than ever to shop around for your ticket. A growing number of budget carriers also offer very competitive prices.

Accommodation. Room rates in top hotels are close if not equal to what you might expect to find in other European capital cities. The approximate price of a double room in high season, in central Warsaw or Kraków: 5-star hotel 500–1,000 zł (US$130–250); 3- to 4-star hotel 400–500 zł (US$100–125); 2-star hotel or pension 250–400 zł (US$65–100).

Meals and drinks. Dining out is a bargain except at the most upmarket and famous restaurants. A three-course meal for two, with wine and service, in a moderately priced restaurant can cost about 120 zł (US$30); at an expensive restaurant, twice that or more.

Local transport. Public transport is inexpensive whether bus, Metro (subway) or tram (4.40 zł). Only taxis are relatively expensive (especially if you wind up in an unofficial taxi). Opt for public transport except in rare instances (after-hours), and always call for a taxi rather than hail one on the street.

Incidentals. Museum admission: around 15–25 zł. Entertainment: theatre, musicals and classical music concerts generally start from 50 zł.

C

CAR HIRE

Hiring a car in Poland isn't a great idea unless you intend to explore the countryside in considerable depth. Car hire is expensive: daily rates in US$, including unlimited mileage, range from $100 a day for an economy-size car, including CDW insurance. At press time, petrol (gas) cost 5zł per litre. Arrangements and conditions for car hire are similar to those in other countries. The minimum age requirement is 21 and you must have been in possession of a valid licence for at least one year. US and Canadian licences are accepted as are international driving licences.

Ask if CDW insurance is included in the price. There are a few local agencies, which tend to be cheaper (though they may not speak English), in addition to the major international agencies, including: Avis (Warsaw, tel: 022 572 6565; Kraków, tel: 012 629 61 08/09; www.avis.pl), Budget (Warsaw, tel: 022 650 4062; www.budget.com.pl), Europcar (Warsaw, tel: 022 650 2564; Kraków, tel: 012 258 12 86; www.europcar.com.pl), Hertz (Warsaw, tel: 022 650 28 96; Kraków, tel: 012 285 50 84; www.hertz.com.pl), and Sixt (Warsaw, tel: 022 650 20 32; Kraków, tel: 012 639 3216; www.pl.sixt.com).

CLIMATE

All of Poland is very cold in winter, and warm but comfortable in summer (it can sometimes be very hot). The best weather (and time to visit) is from May to early June and September to October. Temperatures in the highlands around Zakopane are very cold in winter. The chart below shows the average daytime temperature for Warsaw, in degrees Celsius and Fahrenheit:

	J	F	M	A	M	J	J	A	S	O	N	D
°C	-1	-2	3	12	15	18	17	18	12	12	6	1
°F	30	28	37	54	59	64	63	64	54	54	43	34

CLOTHING

Poles in the big cities tend to be style-conscious, and chic Western fashions are very much in evidence. A jacket and tie would only be suggested at special theatre or opera occasions or very exclusive restaurants. Clothing in the countryside is usually informal.

CRIME AND SAFETY

The country is as safe as most others in the EU and as far as visitors are concerned, the major crime is pickpocketing (usually on buses and trams) or car theft. Take the usual precautions, especially on trips to and from the airport and the railway station, and at night. Thefts have occurred on overnight trains, especially in second-class closed compartments, though the most common occurrence is when boarding. Always be careful in areas frequented by tourists (such as Wawel Hill, Market Square in Kraków).

D

DRIVING

To take your car into Poland you need a valid driving licence and car registration papers. Cars from most European countries (including Britain, Germany and Austria) are presumed to be fully insured, so no extra documentation is needed. To be safe, carry proof of insurance.

Road conditions. Despite recent improvements and the motorway construction, Poland is still a dangerous place to drive your own vehicle as it has one of the highest accident mortality rates in Europe. Narrow country roads leave much to be desired as cars often have to compete with trucks and every other vehicle on the road. An ambitious construction programme involving three major motorways crossing the country (A1, A2 and A4) was well underway at the time of writing. The new motorways are toll-paying, and otherwise driving can be slow-going, especially on popular routes such as that from Kraków up to the Zakopane ski slopes.

Drivers should exercise care, particularly on roads in the countryside, which are often narrow, badly lit at night, and frequently under repair, especially in the summer months. You may find that country roads are used by pedestrians and animals as well as by vehicles. Heavy alcohol consumption can often be a contributing factor in accidents, even given the stringent laws against drinking and driving.

Rules and regulations. Drive on the right and pass on the left, but be careful at all times. Cars must be fitted with a nationality plate or sticker and use headlights at all times, night and day. A set of spare bulbs, a fire extinguisher, a first-aid kit, and a warning triangle are also obligatory. Seat belts are compulsory in front and back seats; children under 12 are prohibited from travelling in the front seat and must be in a car safety seat. Motorcycle riders and passengers must wear crash helmets. Using a mobile phone while driving is prohibited. Drinking and driving laws are tough; a blood alcohol level of more than 0.5 mg per litre is punishable by three years in prison.

Speed limits are 140km/h (87 mph) on motorways, 120km/h (75mph) on dual carriageways, 100km/h (62mph) on single carriageways, 90km/h (56mph) outside urban areas, and 50km/h (31mph) in built-up areas during the daytime and 60km/h (37mph) at night. You may be fined on the spot for speeding.

Fuel costs (benzyna). Petrol (gas) stations are common along highways and main roads, but don't venture down minor roads without filling up. Stations are usually open 24 hours. Unleaded fuel is widely available (about 5 zł) and diesel and LPG are also widely available. Only in the rarest of cases are credit cards not accepted for payment.

Parking. Parking is a problem in any of the big cities, especially where historic centres are pedestrian-only. If you are driving, check that your hotel has parking facilities. A car parked in a prohibited zone will be towed away. Only guarded car parks should be used.

If you need help. If driving your own car, you should take out breakdown insurance cover; car rental companies usually have their own service. For roadside assistance, call the National Roadside Assistance Service, tel: 022 19637. Help will normally arrive within the hour. Three-quarters of breakdowns can be dealt with at the roadside, if you need a tow the charge depends on the type of repair and the towing distance. Remember to put out the red warning triangle 50m (55yd) behind your car or 100m (110yd) behind if you are on a dual carriageway. If anyone is injured, the police must be notified.

Road signs. Standard international pictographs are in use all over Poland. A sign with 'Czarny Punkt', showing a cross in a black circle, indicates a very dangerous area.

E

ELECTRICITY

The current is 220 volts AC, 50 Hertz throughout Poland. Plugs are the standard Continental, round two-pin type, for which British and North American appliances need an adapter. Electrical equipment of 110V/60Hz requires a transformer, though note than most mobile telephone and digital camera chargers incorporate a transformer.

EMBASSIES AND CONSULATES

Embassies are located in Warsaw; a few nations have consulates in other cities, notably Kraków and Gdańsk.

Australia: Embassy, ul. Nowogrodzka 11, tel: 022 521 3444 (www.

australia.pl).

Canada: Embassy, ul. Matejki 1/5, tel: 022 584 3100 (www.canada international.gc.ca/poland-pologne).

Ireland: Embassy (Warsaw), ul. Mysia 5, tel: 022 564 2200 (www.dfa. ie/irish-embassy/poland).

New Zealand: Embassy, Al. Ujazdowskie 51, tel: 022 521 0500 (www.nzembassy.com/poland).

South Africa: Embassy (Warsaw), ul. Koszykowa 54, tel: 022 622 1005 (www.dfa.gov.za).

UK: Embassy, ul. Kawalerii 12, tel: 022 311 0000. Consulate (Kraków), ul. Św. Anny 9, tel: 012 421 7030 (www.gov.uk/government/world/ poland).

USA: Embassy, Al. Ujazdowskie 29/31, tel: 022 504 2000. Consulate (Kraków), ul. Stolarska 9, tel: 012 424 5100 (http://polish.poland. usembassy.gov).

EMERGENCIES

The emergency services telephone numbers are listed below, although the chances of an English speaker at the other end are slim.

Ambulance tel: 999

Fire tel: 998

Police tel: 997

Universal emergency number from a mobile (cell) phone: 112

Between 2 June and 30 September, a special tourist helpline is in operation daily 10am–1pm; tel: 0800 200 300 (from landlines) or 0608 599 999 (from mobile phones).

---

ambulance **karetka pogotowia**
doctor **lekarz**
hospital **szpital**
police **policja**
Can you help me? **Czy może mi pan[i] pomóc?**

GAY AND LESBIAN TRAVELLERS

As a fervently Catholic and conservative country, gay life is not much out in the open in Poland, though an indicator of changing values is that in 2011 Kraków elected Europe's first transgendered member of parliament. Still, there are gay scenes in Warsaw and Kraków and to a lesser extent in smaller cities. A good organisation to contact in Warsaw is Lambda (ul. Żurawia 24A, tel: 022 628 5222, www.lambdawarszawa.org). For information on gay Poland, check out www.gejowo.pl: it's all in Polish but has a countrywide reach and translates well with an internet translation service.

GETTING THERE

Air travel. Many European airlines serve Poland, as do several American and Canadian carriers. In all, Warsaw has flights to and from over 50 cities in more than 30 countries. The Polish national carrier, LOT Polish Airlines, flies from most major European cities and from North America. Scheduled flights are also available from British Airways. From the northeast coast of the US, flying time to Warsaw is about 8 hours.

International airport. Warsaw's Chopin airport is the primary international airport, though there are also international flights to Kraków, Gdańsk, Katowice, Łódź, Szczecin, Poznań, Wrocław and Rzeszow with budget airlines increasing their reach all the time.

Rail travel. Warsaw and Kraków, among other cities, can easily be reached from any major Western, Central or Eastern European city. From the UK, take the Eurostar to Brussels, change for Cologne from which you can take the sleeper to Warsaw, or change in Paris for the sleeper to Berlin, where you can catch an express to Warsaw, Kraków, Poznań, Wrocław or Katowice. InterRail and Eurail passes are valid in Poland. Both RailEurope (www.raileurope.co.uk; tel: 0844 848 40 70) and Deutsche Bahn (www.bahn.com;

tel: 08718 80 80 66) book train journeys across Europe. Warsaw's international railway station is Warszawa Centralna; Kraków's is Dworzec Główny. For train information tel: 042 19 436 (within Poland) or 042 205 55 05 (from outside the country).

By car/coach. Budget airlines may be cheap for those booking ahead, but travelling by coach is still an option, especially if you want to visit several cities – either across Europe or within Poland. Eurolines (www.eurolines.co.uk; tel: 08717 81 81 77 in the UK) has daily departures from London Victoria, changing in Berlin, to all the major cities in Poland and many smaller ones. The trip costs from £40 one way. The Eurolines Pass is also available, for 15 or 30 days from £140. Buses from across Europe arrive at Warszawa Zachodnia (Warsaw West) station (tel: 0703 40 33 30). If you plan to drive across the Continent, the most direct route is via Ostend, Brussels and Berlin.

GUIDES AND TOURS

Travel agencies and organisations in many countries operate organised sightseeing tours of Poland. Look out for specialised trips, such as Jewish pilgrimage tours. Other speciality tours, which you can book on arrival, include Schindler's List tours in Kazimierz, the historic Jewish quarter of Kraków.

H

HEALTH AND MEDICAL CARE

Polish doctors and other health officials are generally knowledgeable and skilled, and most speak some English and German. Doctors and hospitals may expect immediate cash payment for health services although medical treatment will normally be provided free of charge to EU citizens who have a European Health Insurance Card (available from post offices in the UK and online at www.ehic.org.uk). Visitors from non-EU countries should obtain medical insurance, and even EU citizens may wish to insure themselves privately, for example to ensure prompt repatriation in a medical emergency.

Bottled water is inexpensive to buy, although water is safe to drink except perhaps in the deepest countryside. Many Poles drink bottled water because they prefer the taste. If you plan to spend a lot of time in country areas, particularly those close to Russia, Lithuania or Belarus, it is wise to see your doctor about the symptoms and treatment of Lyme disease.

Emergency medical treatment on the scene is available for foreigners. Ask at your hotel or consulate for the name of a doctor who speaks your language. In Warsaw, Kraków, Gdańsk, Katowice, Szczecin, Łódź and Poznań, you can call the private medical service, Falck, using the local city code followed by 19675, which can usually arrange English-language emergency services. Other private hospitals include Centrum Medyczne Damiana (ul. Wałbrzyska 46; tel: 022 566 2222; www.damian.pl) and LUX MED (ul. Puławska 455; tel: 022 431 2059; www.luxmed.pl). Warsaw's Central Emergency Medical Centre is located at ul. Hoża 56 (corner of ul. Poznańska). Centrum Medicover (tel: 500 900 500; www.medicover.pl) has medical centres in various Polish cities, such as Kraków, Warsaw, Poznań and Gdańsk; in emergencies tel: 500 900 999 (24 hours).

Pharmacies. Look for the sign 'apteka'. In Poland these shops only sell pharmaceutical and related products. Tourism Information Offices have lists of night pharmacies. In Warsaw, two are: Apteka Przy Willowej (ul. Puławska 39, tel: 022 849 3757) and Apteka Grabowskiego (al. Jerozolimskie 54, Centralny Station, tel: 022 825 6986). Local editions of In Your Pocket (www.inyourpocket.com), list additional pharmacies.

Where's the nearest pharmacy? **Gdzie jest najbliższa apteka?**
I need a doctor. **Ja potrzebuję doktora.**
I need a dentist. **Ja potrzebuję dentystę.**

L

LANGUAGE

Polish, a Slavic language, is the mother tongue of 99 percent of the population. The most widely known foreign language is English ahead of Russian and German. Young people in large cities are most likely to speak one or even two foreign languages, but communication can be troublesome with elders and in the countryside. In the cities English speakers are unlikely to find many problems. In the countryside, communication difficulties are to be expected. The Polish language is grammatically complicated, but at least it is written completely phonetically. Learning even a handful of key phrases is a good idea and will prove helpful. As a general rule, stress falls on the second-last syllable.

The following are a few useful phrases and some signs you are likely to see:

yes **tak**
no **nie**
Hi. (informal, singular/plural) **Cześć (chesh).**
Good night. **Dobranoc.**
Goodbye. **Do widzenia.**
Thank you (very much). **Dziękuję (bardzo).**
Excuse me (sorry). **Przepraszam.**
Do you speak English? **Czy Pan/Pani mówi po angielsku?**
I don't understand. **Nie rozumiem.**
I understand. **Rozumiem.**
I don't know. **Nie wiem.**
Where is...? **Gdzie jest...?**
How do I get to...? **Jak dojechać do...?**
Good morning/day. **Dzień dobry. (jen doe-bri)**
Good evening. **Dobry wieczór. (do-bri vee-a ye-chor)**

Please. **Proszę. (pro-sha)**
Help! **Pomocy! (po-mo-tsay)**
Where is the toilet? **Gdzie są toalety?**
May I have...? **Czy mogę...?**
entrance **wejście**
exit **wyjście**
open **otwarte / czynne**
closed **zamknięte**
pharmacy **apteka**
post office **poczta**
avenue **Aleja (Al.)**
street **ulica (ul.)**
city centre **centrum**
old town **Stare Miasto**

M

MAPS

Tourism Information Offices (see page 175) routinely supply visitors with free maps of cities (and regions, often for a nominal fee) that are sufficient for most peoples' purposes. There are plenty of more comprehensive maps available, published by PPWK and others. Those driving through Poland may want to purchase a Road Atlas (Atlas Samochodowy).

MEDIA

Newspapers and magazines. *The Warsaw Voice* (www.warsawvoice. pl), published weekly, is probably the most authoritative English-language newspaper. It gives a good insight into Polish politics, business and culture and also has a listings section for tourists. Other papers to look for include *Welcome to Warsaw* (a free information magazine), *Warsaw Insider* (www.warsawinsider.pl) a free monthly with cultural listings, Culture.pl website an authoritative guide to Polish culture and the ever-growing series of *In Your Pocket* mini-guides which have lots of listings and opinionated information (Warsaw, Kraków, Gdańsk, Wrocław, Łódź and Poznań editions at differing intervals, also available as iPhone apps). *Kraków Post* (www.krakowpost.com) is an entertaining monthly. Western newspapers, including *The International Herald Tribune*, *Financial Times*, *The Guardian* and *USA Today*, arrive the day of publication.

Radio and television. Polskie Radio (www.thenews.pl) is transmitted in English streamed over the internet and as podcasts. Even quite modest hotels now offer satellite television with major European and American channels and news programmes.

MONEY

Currency. The unit of currency is the złoty (zł). Coins in circulation include 1, 2 and 5 zł. Banknotes come in denominations of 10, 20, 50, 100 and 200 zł. One złoty equals 100 groszy (gr), which you'll see in 1, 2, 5, 10, 20 and 50 coin denominations.

Currency exchange. Foreign currency can be exchanged (look for the signs marked *kantor*) at the airports and banks, as well as most hotels. *Kantors* only exchange cash and can be very informal-looking places. They offer the best rates (no commission). Your passport is only necessary when changing money at banks. The exchange rate at the time of writing is around 3.9 zł to the US dollar and 6.1 zł to the pound. There is no black market for currency in Poland; any offers from strangers to exchange money should be refused as this will be counterfeit. The Polish word for cash is *gotówka*.

Numbers	
zero **zero**	three **trzy**
one **jeden**	four **cztery**
two **dwa / dwie**	five **pięć**

six **sześć**	seventeen **siedemnaście**
seven **siedem**	eighteen **osiemnaście**
eight **osiem**	nineteen **dziewiętnaście**
nine **dziewięć**	twenty **dwadzieścia**
ten **dziesięć**	thirty **trzydzieści**
eleven **jedenaście**	forty **czterdzieści**
fifteen **piętnaście**	fifty **pięćdziesiąt**
sixteen **szesnaście**	hundred **sto**

Credit cards. Major international credit cards (Visa, MasterCard and American Express) are accepted in most hotels, restaurants and shops.

ATMs. Cash machines (bankomat), taking PLUS, Cirrus and most other major credit cards, are widespread in Polish cities and offer competitive international exchange rates. They dispense cash in Polish zł; some also give cash in euros.

Travellers cheques. These may be cashed at all of the above outlets except *kantors* and may sometimes be substituted for cash, but you'll almost certainly get a much poorer rate of exchange than if you convert them to cash. Commission is generally 1 to 2 percent.

O

OPENING TIMES

Opening times vary, but most businesses in Poland are open 8am–5pm Monday to Friday. Supermarkets, department stores and shopping centres are open 9am–8pm, Monday to Saturday; Sunday, 10am–6pm and sometimes later. Smaller shops are open 10am–6pm Monday to Friday, 9 or 10am–11 or 12 noon Saturday. Some close all day Saturday, and almost all shut on Sunday. 'Non-Stop' signs mean 24-hour shopping.

Banks are generally open 9am–6pm Monday to Friday. Museums

are usually closed on Monday, and are open 10am–5pm Tuesday to Sunday, but museum hours can vary enormously with some closing for lunch and others with opening hours that change monthly.

P

POLICE *(policja)* (see also Crime & Safety and Emergencies)
Police emergency, tel: 997 or 112 from a mobile.
Warsaw Police Headquarters: ul.Puławska 148/150 (tel: 022 621 02 51).

police station **posterunek policji**

POST OFFICES *(poczta)*
The Central Post Office (Urząd Pocztowy Warszawa 1) in Warsaw (ul. Świętokrzyska 31–33, tel: 022 505 3400) is open 24 hours a day. Other useful branches are at Targowa Street (ul. Targowa 73, also 24 hours a day, tel: 022 590 0313), on ul. Marszałkowska 26 (Mon–Fri 8am–8.30pm; tel: 022 629 3226) and Old Market Square (Rynek Starego Miasta 15, 8am–8pm Mon–Fri, Sat 9am–4pm; tel: 022 831 0281).

In Kraków, the main Post Office is just east of the Planty (ul. Westerplatte 20, tel: 012 421 44 89; open Mon–Fri 8am–8.30pm, Sat 8am–3pm). For post out of hours try the branch opposite the train station at (ul. Lubicz 4; tel: 012 422 91 68; open 24 hours for stamps, post and money transfers).

International postcards and letters to Europe as well as the rest of the world cost 5.20 zł.

DHL, TNT and UPS all have offices in Warsaw and in Kraków.

letter **list**
stamp **znaczek**
air mail **poczta lotnicza**

PUBLIC HOLIDAYS
1 January New Year's Day
6 January Epiphany
March/April Easter Sunday and Easter Monday
1 May Labour Day
3 May Constitution Day
May/June Pentecost (7th Sunday after Easter)
June Corpus Christi (9th Thursday after Easter)
15 August Feast of the Assumption
1 November All Saints' Day
11 November Independence Day
25 December Christmas Day
26 December St Stephen's Day

R

RELIGION
Nearly all native Poles declare themselves as Roman Catholic, but only 39 percent are practising Catholics. The late Pope John Paul II was a Cardinal and Archbishop of Kraków before becoming the head of the Catholic Church. Mass is said in Polish.

Other minority faiths, notably Protestant, Eastern Orthodox and Jewish, are represented in Poland. Tourism Information Offices should have a list of services held in English and other languages (infrequent).

T

TELEPHONES *(telefon)*
Public telephones. Public telephones are rare in Poland. If you can actually find one, it works using prepaid cards bought from any shop or kiosk selling sweets and cigarettes.
Mobile phones. Avoid roaming costs by putting a local prepaid SIM

card in your mobile phone. Several companies now offer start-up packages for less than 10zł, with top-up cards costing 5zł and upwards. Both can be bought from shops and kiosks around the city as well as the airport, bus and railway stations.

Making the call. To call Poland from outside the country, dial your international access code followed by 48 for Poland and the subscriber number minus the initial 0. If you're calling within the country on a landline you simply dial the 10-digit number include the area code beginning with 0. The same applies for calling a landline from a Polish mobile with the exception of Plus GSM, which requires the dropping of the first 0. To get a line out of Poland, dial 00 plus the country code. Mobile telephone numbers have 10 digits.

International dialling code for Poland: 48
Local and regional directory assistance: 118 913
International directory assistance: 118 912
Area codes:
Gdańsk/Gdynia/Sopot 058
Kraków 012
Łodź 042
Poznań 061
Toruń 056 / 055
Warsaw 022
Zakopane 018
Zamość 084

TIME ZONE

All of Poland is in the same time zone, Central European Time, or Greenwich Mean Time + 1 hour (or US Eastern Standard Time + 6 hours). As in the rest of Europe, the clocks go forward one hour on the last Sunday of March and back again on the last Sunday of October.

New York	London	**Warsaw**	Jo'burg	Sydney	Auckland
6am	11am	**noon**	1pm	10pm	midnight

TIPPING

Tipping is the norm in Poland but not obligatory. It's customary to leave 10–15 percent at restaurants and round up the bill at bars. Some restaurants may add on a 10 percent tip. Porters, maids and tourist guides also expect tips.

> bill/check **rachunek**

TOILETS

In Poland public toilets (toaleta publiczna) can be few and far between. A small charge (1–2 zł) is common, and even cafés (especially at petrol stations) may still charge patrons for use of their facilities. Men's rooms are commonly denoted by triangle symbols; women's rooms are denoted by circles.

> men's room **męski (panowie)**
> women's restroom **damski (panie)**
> free **wolny**
> occupied **zajęty**

TOURIST INFORMATION

Polish tourist information centres range from desks tucked away in the corners of obliging travel agencies, to dedicated buildings complete with interactive maps. The most popular tourist cities such as Kraków, Warsaw and Gdańsk have many branches. Note that there is a difference between official tourist information centres and the many agencies that label themselves 'tourist information' and exist mainly to sell guided tours and tickets. As well as being able to help you plan your itinerary, most places also offer help and advice on accommodation, car hire, the best places to eat authentic local food as well as a whole host of other useful services. Below are details of a few of the tourist information offices in the key cities.

Warsaw. You will find tourist information points at Chopin Airport (Terminal A, exit 2); Palace of Culture and Science (pl. Defilad 1, from ul. Emilii Plater, between Kongresowa Hall and Museum of Technology); Warszawa Centralna (the Central Railway Station's main hall); Rynek Starego Miasta 19–21a and Kordegarda (ul. Krakowski Przedmieście 15–17). For general tourist information, tel: 022 19431 or see www.warsawtour.pl.

Kraków. The offical Krakow City Tourist Office has several InfoKraków branches throughout the city, mainly open daily 9am–7pm. Cloth Hall, Main Market Square 1-3 (tel: 012 433 73 10; www.krakow.pl).

Gdańsk. Again, there are several Centrum Informacji Turystycznej, at the airport and in the city: ul. Długi Targ 28–29 (058 301 4355, www.gdansk4u.pl); ul. Długa 45 (tel: 058 301 1343; www.pttk-gdansk.pl) and others, www.gdansk.pl.

Łódź. Centrum Informacji Turystycznej (ul. Piotrkowska 87, tel: 042 638 5956/55), http://pl.cit.lodz.pl), at the airport and other points in the city.

Poznań. Centrum Informacji Miejskiej (ul. Ratajczaka 44, tel: 061 19431 or 061 851 9645) and Tourism Information Centre (Stary Rynek 59-60, tel: 061 852 6156), www.poznan.pl.

Wrocław Tourist Information Centre (Rynek 14, 51-101 Wrocław tel. 071 3443 111, www.wroclaw-info.pl

Official web addresses for other destinations listed in this book:

Auschwitz www.auschwitz.org

Kazimierz Dolny www.kazimierzdolny.pl

Malbork www.visitmalbork.pl

Sopot www.sopot.pl

Toruń www.torun.pl

Wieliczka www.wieliczka.eu

Zakopane www.promocja.zakopane.pl

Zamość www.zamosc.pl

UK: Polish National Tourist Office, Westgate House, West Gate, London W5 1YY; tel: 0300 303 1812; www.poland.travel.
US: Polish National Tourist Office, 5 Marine View Plaza, Hoboken, New Jersey, NJ 07030; tel: 201 420 99 10; www.poland.travel.

TRANSPORT
Local transport
Most Polish cities have well-developed systems of public transport that include buses and trams (and in the case of Warsaw, two Metro, or subway, lines).

In Warsaw (www.ztm.waw.pl), buses run from 5am to 11.30pm; night buses from 11.15pm to 4.30am. Tickets (valid on buses, trams and the Metro) can be purchased at kiosks with a green-and-yellow Ruch logo, and you can also buy a ticket directly from the driver for a slightly higher price or at vending machines on buses and trams. Lines beginning with the number 1, 2, or 3 stop at all stops, those beginning 4 and 5 are speedier.

In Kraków, there are many tram lines and many more bus lines (www.mpk.krakow.pl). They run from 5am to 11pm. You can purchase single-trip tickets, one-hour tickets, one-day and one-week passes. Some night buses (numbers always start with 6) run about once an hour from midnight mostly through the city centre (they stop under the Central Station).

Buses (autobus). Validate your ticket upon boarding to avoid an on-the-spot fine. There is a wide range of ticket prices, with time-limited tickets allowing passengers to change lines within the stated time. Signal that you want to get off by pressing the bell. Roadworks and the rapid modernisation of Polish cities mean that routes are subject to change.

Trams (tramwaj). Trams, or streetcars, cover large networks in most Polish cities; some run throughout the night. At peak hours tram is the fastest way (other than the metro) to get around large Polish cities, which are usually backed up in traffic jams.

Taxis (taksówka). Taxi fares depend on the length of the journey and the rate, which changes according to the time of day. Night and weekend rates are higher. Official licensed taxis are clearly badged inside and out and have a roof-light. The driver should switch on the meter at the beginning of the journey and give you a receipt on payment. However there are cases of foreigners being over-charged, especially since most drivers only speak Polish. Unofficial taxis are common, and tend to gather at airports and train stations. If you want a taxi, ask your hotel to call one for you. For taxi com-pany details, see page 157. Hailing a cab is not recommended.

Subway or underground (Metro). The Metro in Warsaw (www. metro.waw.pl) operates two lines. One runs through the city cen-tre from Młociny station to the southern suburb of Kabaty (near Ursynów) and another one from Rondo Daszyńskiego (east of the city centre) to Dworzec Wileński on the other side of the Vistula river. It functions daily 5am–midnight (to 3am Fri and Sat), with trains every 3–4 minutes during rush hour, every 8 minutes during off-peak hours.

Transport around the country

Buses/coaches (autobus). The main bus station in Warsaw is War-szawa Zachodnia (Warsaw West, Al. Jerozolimskie 144, tel: 0703 403 330). Kraków's main bus station is behind the train station (ul Bosacka 18, tel: 012 411 8019). Gdańsk's bus station is Dworzec PKS (ul. 3 Maja 12, tel: 58 306 48 43) adjacent to the train station.

The national bus service PKS (www.pksbilety.pl) has the most extensive network of bus routes throughout the country.

For bus information, tel: 708-208-888.

Trains (pociąg). With more than 26,500km (16,450 miles) of railway lines, the Polish railway network covers the whole country, making trains by far the most common and best way to travel between major cities. The exception is short journeys, when buses can be faster (Kraków to Zakopane, for example). Warsaw has three big railway stations; most international trains arrive at Warszawa Centralna

(Al. Jerozolimskie 54), while others go to Warszawa Zachodnia (Al. Jerozolimskie 144), which has good interchanges and Warszawa Wschodnia (ul. Lubelska 1) across the river in Praga. Smaller stations, mostly on the edges of the city, handle regional routes.

Kraków's main railway station is Kraków Dworzec Główny (Pl. Dworcowy 1, tel: 012 9436); it handles international and inter-city routes. Gdańsk's railway station is Gdańsk Główny (ul. Podwale Grodzkie 1, tel: 058 9436); the fast SKM commuter train connects the Tri-city area, leaving every 10 minutes between 6am and 7.30pm and less frequently thereafter.

The rail journey from Warsaw to Kraków takes 2 hours 25 minutes; from Warsaw to Gdańsk, 3 hours; and from Warsaw to Poznań, 2hours 28 minutes (fast trains).

Tickets can be purchased at the train station in advance or on board from the conductor (for a surcharge).

For train timetables and information, visit http://pkp.pl, www. intercity.pl. Informaton: tel: 22 19757; from abroad: 48 42 20 55 007).

railway station **dworzec kolejowy**
bus stop **przystanek**
ticket kiosk (buses/trams) **sprzedaż biletów mpk**
reserved seat ticket **miejscówka**
departure **odjazd**
arrival **przyjazd**
Please, a ticket to... **Proszę bilet do...**
return ticket **bilet powrotny**

V

VISAS AND ENTRY REQUIREMENTS

All visitors need a valid passport to enter Poland. Holders of European Union passports do not need a visa and may stay as long as they please. Visitors holding passports from many other countries, including Australia, New Zealand, Canada and the US may also enter Poland without a visa but their stay may be limited, usually for 90 days. Citizens of South Africa and a few other states will need a visa; check at www.msz.gov.pl. Poland is a member of the Schengen group of countries, meaning that a Schengen Block visa is valid for entry to Poland. Visa applications need to be registered online at www.e-konsulat.gov.pl, where there is more detailed visa information. Minimum visa processing times range from 10 days to a month, depending on the passport held, and can take longer.

Customs restrictions. There is a 10,000-euro limit on the amount of currency you can bring into Poland. Visitors are allowed to bring in duty-free alcohol and tobacco products for personal use only, eg, 800 cigarettes and 10 litres of spirits. Check with your home country how much you can bring back duty-free from Poland. Note that airport checks are fierce. Call Customs Information hotline at 801 470 477 for details.

There are also strict regulations to prevent the export of objects of national heritage, such as works of art and antiques. In most cases, works by living artists and works less than 55 years old are exempt. However, there are exceptions to this rule. Reputable antique and art dealers can help their clients get export permits from the Ministry of Culture and National Heritage. Each region has its own department for the export of works of art. In Warsaw it is: Wojewódzki Urząd Ochrony Zabytków W Warszawie, ul. Nowy Świat 18/20; tel: 022 443 04 40; www.mwkz.pl.

W

WEBSITES AND INTERNET ACCESS

Most cafés, especially in the city centres, as well as hotels and hostels offer free wi-fi.

In Kraków, travellers can access free wi-fi in and around the

Main Market Square (Rynek Główny). The municipal hot spot network has been recently extended to more than 21 points across the city. Look out, too, for the hotspot Cracovia logo signalling free wi-fi at hotels and cafés.

Warsaw has free internet hot spots in the Old Town, on Krakowskie Przedmieście Street, 'Wiech' Passage (pasaż Wiecha) at the back of the 'Wars i Sawa' Shopping Centre and in the area of Browarna Street (Powiśle district). Free connection is widely available in the city centre. You can check the map of free wi-fi points at www.warsawtour.pl. Free internet access is also available in many cafés and on some buses.

Here are some useful websites to help you plan your trip to Poland:

www.poland.travel (Polish National Tourist Office)

www.polishworld.com (general information, news, culture)

www.warsawvoice.com.pl (site of English-language weekly)

www.inyourpocket.com (In Your Pocket listings site)

www.krakow.pl (Kraków site)

www.warsawtour.pl (Warsaw tourist information)

www.gdansk.pl (municipal site)

www.destinationwarsaw.com (general information about the city)

Y

YOUTH HOSTELS

There is an extensive network of youth hostels *(schroniska młod-zieżowe)* – reportedly as many as 950 in all – throughout Poland. For information, contact the Polish Association of Youth Hostels (ul. Mokotowska 14, Warsaw, tel: 022 849 8128, www.ptsm.org.pl). International Student Hostels Accommodation is available through the ALMATUR Travel Bureau (ul. Kopernika 23, Warsaw, tel: 022 826 2639, www.almatur.pl). In the main tourist cities, you will also find excellent privately-run hostels, which are a good choice for travellers on a budget.

RECOMMENDED HOTELS

Accommodation for visitors to Poland has improved greatly in recent years, with hotels offering modern facilities, often in beautiful old buildings. However, especially at the mid- to lower-range, choices can be limited. International chains and joint ventures have moved in to replace the former state-run chains that were, not always successfully, privatised, and some new, small, Polish-owned private chains are offering excellent quality. It is always wise to book ahead, particularly for June, July, August and September.

The following guide denotes the rack rate price of a double room with bath/shower in high season (May through October, as well as Christmas) including breakfast and VAT. Hotel room rates are variously quoted in US dollars, euros and Polish złoty – though the bill will ultimately be rendered in złoty. Hotels do not always include breakfast in the price they quote on websites, etc, so you will need to check when booking. All accept major credit cards, except where noted.

Most local tourism information offices will also have lists of private accommodation.

$$$$	over 600zł
$$$	425–600zł
$$	250–425zł
$	below 250zł

KRAKÓW

Cybulskiego Guest Rooms $ *ul. Cybulskiego 6, tel: 012 423 05 32,* www. freerooms.pl. A short walk from Rynek Główny, this is a simple, well-run set of rooms and small apartments, all with private bathrooms and kitchenettes, that has a cheerful cellar breakfast room.

Grand Hotel $$$$ *ul. Sławkowska 5/7, tel: 012 424 0800,* www.grand. pl. A stylish 19th-century Old Town hotel with stained-glass shining on its hallways and classic furnishings, the Grand is one of the most impressive places to stay in Kraków. It offers lavishly furnished rooms and some extremely chic suites with period features. There are two elegant restaurants, a café/bar and elegant club & bar.

Wielopole Hotel $ *ul. Wielopole 3, tel: 012 422 1475*, www.wielopole. pl. Excellent value accommodation two minutes east of the Old Town; facilities are clean and modern. Prices include free high-speed internet connection in every room.

Hotel Copernicus $$$$ *ul. Kanonicza 16, tel: 012 424 3400*, www.hotel. com.pl. On one of Kraków's most atmospheric streets, this is one of the city's grandest hotels. It integrates all modern facilities (including a swimming pool in the vaults) in a marvellously restored 16th-century building just minutes from Wawel Hill. Rooms are elegant, furnished with well-chosen antiques. Breakfast not included.

Hotel Eden $$ *ul. Ciemna 15, tel: 012 430 6565*, www.hoteleden.pl. A friendly, small hotel leading a revival of the historic Jewish quarter, Kazimierz. Simple and modern furnishings in a renovated 15th-century building, with a salt-cave sauna, mikvah (Jewish ritual bath) and offering groups who pre-book kosher food.

Hotel Francuski $$ *ul. Pijarska 13, tel: 012 627 3777*, http://hotel-francuski-krakow.h-rez.com. This handsome, traditional hotel, built in 1912, is on the edge of the Old Town, facing the Planty near the old city wall and the Czartoryski Museum and three minutes' walk from the Rynek. It has a long-standing reputation for luxury and elegance. Wheelchair access.

Hotel Maltański $$ *ul. Straszewskiego 14, tel: 012 431 0010*, www.doni mirski.com. One of a small, boutique hotel chain, this modern and elegant hotel in a renovated 19th-century building is in a quiet location on the southwestern edge of the Planty within walking distance of Wawel Hill and all major sights. Classy rooms, good service and breakfast.

Hotel Pollera $$ *ul. Szpitalna 30, tel: 012 422 1044*, www.pollera.com.pl. Art lovers will like this traditional 150-year-old hotel the moment they enter the lobby. A stained-glass window by Kraków artist Stanislaw Wyspiański hangs over the staircase. Rooms are old-fashioned but nicely equipped for the price. Close to the Opera House and Market Square.

Hotel Polski $$ *ul. Pijarska 17, tel: 012 422 1144,* www.donimirski. com. A pleasant, medium-sized, quiet hotel, near St Florian's Gate, with wi-fi and all mod cons, yet proud of its historic inheritance, from the fossils in the lobby floor to its 19th-century friezes.

Hotel Rezydent $$ *ul. Grodzka 9, tel: 012 429 5410,* www.rezydent.kra- kow.pl. A great location if you want to be in the thick of things: on the street with the most foot traffic leading off the Market Square. Appropriately ancient on the outside, fresh and modern on the inside. Triples and a huge apartment for four available.

Hotel Saski $$$ *ul. Sławkowska 3, tel: 012 421 4222,* www.hotelsaski. com.pl. An enviably located old-style hotel in a 16th century building, smack in the middle of the Old Town, on one of its nicest streets. Rooms are either very traditional and very frilly, or rather modern.

NorPol Apartments $$$ *ul. Szlak 50/115, tel: 512 265 271,* http://nor pol-apartments.com. A range of good-looking, non-smoking apart- ments from matchbox-size to palaces throughout the city centre, which offer a range of add-ons, including airport pick-up and day trips. Long-term rental is also available. A good choice for anyone looking for self-catering.

Pod Róża $$$$ *ul. Floriańska 14, tel: 012 424 3300,* www.podroza.hotel. com.pl. One of Kraków's most popular Old Town hotels is this mid-size charmer in the centre of everything. The 14th-century building has been renovated in a traditional old-fashioned style, keeping the arched ceil- ings and chandeliers, adding modern technology where necessary.

Pod Wawelem $$ *pl. Na Groblach 22, tel: 012 426 2626,* www.hotel podwawelem.pl. Simple yet comfortable accommodation in a modern building with friendly, helpful staff is made special by its stunning riv- erside location at the foot of Wawel hill, within easy walking distance of both the Old Town and Kazimierz. In summer the rooftop bar offers an unparalleled view.

Stary $$$$ *ul. Szczepańska 5, tel: 012 384 0808,* www.stary.hotel.com. pl. Everything is impeccable here, from the blend of 14th-century and contemporary style, to the service. A rooftop bar with a splendid view of the Rynek provides a wonderful place to unwind in the summer.

Hotel Belvedere $$$ *ul. Droga do Białego 3, tel: 018 202 0255,* www. belvederehotel.pl. Modern hotel built in the traditional, local style, with a sports centre including a swimming pool, squash court and gym. Three restaurants, a café and two bars provide plenty of choice. Within walking distance of Zakopane's centre.

Hotel Litwor $$–$$$ *ul. Krupówki 40, tel: 018 202 4200,* www.litwor. pl. On a small square off Zakopane's main shopping promenade, this large, handsome traditional hotel is one of the choicest places to stay in town. It has a delightful lobby bar, great restaurant, nicely furnished rooms, an indoor swimming pool and fitness centre with sauna.

Hotel Art & Spa $$$$ *ul. Kosciuszki 18, tel: 018 200 0670,* www.artand-spa.pl. A traditional, elegant country-house hotel in a central location, with a wellness and spa centre. The restaurant serves excellent Polish and European cuisine.

Arkadia $ *Rynek Wielki 9, tel: 084 638 6507,* www.arkadia-zamosc. com.pl. An enviable location, right on one of Poland's finest Renaissance market squares, this tiny hotel offers wi-fi and excellent value.

Mercure Zamość Stare Miasto $$ *ul. Kołłątaja 2–6, tel: 084 639 2516,* www.accorhotels.com. This hotel, occupying six nicely renovated 16th-century townhouses next to the Town Hall on the magnificent Market Square is part of the Accor chain and is one of its better efforts. Stylishly modern, but respectful of the original architecture, the buildings are connected by lovely interior courtyards.

Dom Architekta $$ *Rynek 20, tel: 081 883 5544,* http://domarchitekta sarp.pl. Owned by the Polish Union of Architects, who have taken a minimal approach to traditional style, in a great location on the Market Square. Breakfast included in room price.

Hotel Zajazd Piastowski $ *ul. Słoneczna 3, tel: 081 889 0900,* www. zajazdpiastowski.pl. A large and pleasant chalet-style hotel, set in countryside a few kilometres beyond the town centre. Swimming pool and bicycle rental, horseback riding.

Willa Agnieszka $ *ul. Krakowska 41 A, tel: 081 882 0411,* www.willa agnieszka.pl. Handily placed for the Rynek yet in leafy surroundings, this modern villa has its own restaurant. A couple of suites have fireplaces, and others balconies overlooking the river. The decor is not the most successful modern take on Polish traditional style.

WARSAW

Agrykola $ *ul. Myśliwiecka 9, tel: 022 622 9110,* www.agrykola-noclegi. pl. This good value hostel near the Łazienki Park and the Ujazdowski Castle is aimed primarily at student sports groups and offers simple accommodation about 3km from the city centre.

Hotel Campanile $$ *ul. Towarowa 2, tel: 022 582 7200,* www.camp anile.com.pl. Inside the same huge building as two other hotels, the city-centre air-conditioned Campanile is benefitting from an upgrade taking place throughout the chain. It may be characterless, but for value, service and facilities this one really is very hard to beat.

Hotel Harenda $$ *Krakowskie Przedmieście 4–6, tel: 022 826 0071,* www.hotelharenda.com.pl. Great location near the university on one of Warsaw's finest streets, a few minutes' walk from the Old Town. Rooms are modern and plainly furnished. There's a lively pub (of the same name) next door.

Hotel Maria $$$ *al. Jana Pawła II 71, tel: 022 838 4062,* www.hotelmaria. pl. A delightful family-run hotel near the Powązki and Jewish cemeteries and within walking distance of the Old Town. Friendly service and nicely furnished modern rooms; an especially good option for those who don't like big corporate hotels. The restaurant offers a good variety of Polish and European dishes and a well-chosen wine list.

Hotel Bristol $$$$ *ul. Krakowskie Przedmieście 42–4, tel: 022 551 1000,* www.hotelbristolwarsaw.pl. The most luxurious traditional hotel in Warsaw, this beautiful 1901 Beaux Arts building is elegantly furnished throughout. Within walking distance of the Old Town. Fitness centre, pool, sauna. Great café, restaurant.

Marriott Warsaw $$$-$$$$ *al. Jerozolimskie 65–79, tel: 022 630 6306,* www.marriott.com. Luxurious modern high-rise in the city centre, with 10 restaurants, health club, swimming pool and penthouse cocktail bar.

MDM Hotel $$$ *pl. Konstytucji 1, tel: 022 339 1600,* www.hotelmdm. com.pl. Large hotel centrally located on Constitution Square. The building is typical of 1950s Polish architecture, and the standard décor is rather anonymous, but rooms are large and it's a fair deal for the location.

Nathan's Villa $ *ul. Piękna 24–6, tel: 022 622 2946,* www.nathansvilla hostel.pl. This small hostel chain has acquired a legendary status. Accommodation is simple, modern and neat as you'd expect, but, best of all, it's right in the heart of town, just off the main Marszałkowska drag.

Polonia Palace Hotel $$$ *al. Jerozolimskie 45, tel: 022 318 2800,* www. poloniapalace.com. One of Warsaw's oldest hotels, immaculately restored with a Belle Époque restaurant and modern facilities, in a city centre location.

Sheraton Warsaw $$$$ *ul. Prusa 2, tel: 022 450 6100,* www.sheraton. com.pl. The hotel of choice for international business travellers, the very modern and elegant Sheraton is located halfway between Łazienki Park and the Old Town. Rooms are luxuriously appointed, and 'executive rooms' are completely outfitted with work facilities. Excellent gym, restaurants, services.

GDANSK

Dom Aktora $$ *ul. Straganiarska 55–56, tel: 058 301 5901,* www.dom aktora.pl. This low-key pension in the heart of the Main Town has a reputation as a boarding house for actors and theatre people. Rooms are utterly simple, but very clean and the art on the walls is for sale.

Hotel Hanza $$$$ *ul. Tokarska 6, tel: 058 305 3427,* www.hotel hanza.pl. One of Gdańsk's most luxurious options in the Main Town. On the waterfront (some rooms have river views), this modern hotel is also just minutes from the Long Market. Attractive and luxurious rooms with a clean aesthetic décor. Hairdressing salon and fitness centre with spa. Very good restaurant and cocktail bar.

Mercure Gdańsk Stare Miasto $$$ *ul. Heweliusza 22, tel: 058 321 0000,* www.mercure.com. Within walking distance of the Old Town, this comfortable modern hotel has a good restaurant, beauty salon, massage parlour, solarium and nightclub. Being a highrise, the hotel provides great views from the guestrooms.

Minihotel Abak $ *ul. Beethovena 8, tel: 058 306 2990,* www.abak. gda.pl. A bit of a trek from the city centre up a long steep hill, this superb value guesthouse provides clean, albeit basic accommodation with a communal kitchen and the facility to have restaurant food delivered to your room. Possibly the best budget option in the city.

Scandic Hotel Gdańsk $$$$ *ul. Podwale Grodzkie 9, tel: 058 300 6000,* www.scandichotels.com. This large chain hotel (formerly the Holiday Inn) is just across from the Gdańsk railway station, and close to the highlights of the Main Town, the Old Town and the now-quiet shipyards. Good service, quality business facilities, standard but well-equipped Scandinavian-style rooms.

SOPOT

Pensjonat Wanda $–$$ *ul. Poniatowskiego 7, tel: 058 550 3037,* www. bws-hotele.pl. Perfectly located by the beach and near the pier, this pension occupies a period building, with sauna and solarium, and has its own restaurant. Room service is also available

Sofitel Grand Hotel $$$ *ul. Powstancóv Warszawy 12–14, tel: 058 520 6000,* www.sofitel.com. Most appropriately named, this impressive red-roofed hotel, a 1927 Art Nouveau landmark, sits facing the Gdańsk Bay in the chic seaside resort of Sopot. The hotel is refined but not pretentious. A surprisingly good deal.

Hotel Petite Fleur $–$$ *ul. Piekary 25, tel: 056 621 5100,* www.petite
fleur.pl. A cosy little hotel in the heart of Toruń's Old Town. The accommodation is spread over two elegant Renaissance burgher's
houses and has retained numerous period features. Rooms are
large and comfortable. Very good restaurant downstairs in the cellar.

Hotel Zajazd Staropolski $$ *ul. Żeglarska 10–14, tel: 056 622 6060,*
www.zajazd-gromada.pl. One of the best options in the Old Town,
between the Copernicus Museum and St Mary's Church. Comfort-
able and pet-friendly. Well-equipped rooms, with simple, modern
furniture are spread between three handsome townhouses. Good
restaurant too.

Mleczarnia Hostel $ *Ul. Włodkowica 5, tel: 071 787 75 70*, www.mlec-
zarniahostel.pl. Well located hostel whose ground floor is given over
to one of the liveliest bars in the city. Dorms are clean, bathrooms
equally so and there is a range of private rooms with en-suites too.

Mercure Panorama $$ Pl. Dominikański 1, tel: 071 323 27 00, www.
mercure.com. In the city centre; 70 double rooms, 34 single rooms,
8 apartments – all with bathroom/WC, satellite TV; restaurant, café,
dancing, dogs allowed, guarded car park.

Brovaria $$ *Stary Rynek 73–4, tel: 061 858 6868,* www.brovaria.pl.
With views over the Old Market Square, this hotel combines stylish
modernity with historic architecture. Good restaurant and bar.

Hotel Royal $$ *ul. Św. Marcina 71, tel: 061 858 2300,* www.hotel-royal.
com.pl. Set back from the busy shopping street of Św. Marcina in
a quiet courtyard, this exceedingly handsome hotel is within easy
walking distance of the Old Town. The staff are friendly and the
rooms are large.

INDEX

Berlitz POCKET GUIDE

POLAND

Fifth Edition 2016
Editor: Kate Drynan
Author: Neil Schlecht
Head of Production: Rebeka Davies
Picture Editor: Tom Smyth
Cartography Update: Carte
Update Production: AM Services
Photography Credits: Bigstock 27; Corrie
Wingate/Apa Publications 4TL, 6ML, 9, 40, 51,
55, 56, 58, 61, 62, 63, 64, 128, 141, 146; Getty
Images 25, 29, 30, 80, 88; Gregory Wrona/Apa
Publications 5MC, 6MC, 6TL, 6TL, 7M, 7M, 8R,
9R, 15, 17, 37, 38, 42, 46, 48, 52, 68, 70, 75, 76,
86, 91, 102, 104, 106, 109, 113, 122, 132, 134,
136, 140, 142, 145; iStock 4MC, 5T, 5M, 6ML,
7T, 7TC, 8L, 10, 13, 32, 35, 44, 65, 67, 72, 79,
82, 84, 85, 92, 94, 95, 97, 98, 133, 138; Kaplan
Productions 23; Public domain 20; Shutterstock
4TC, 4ML, 5TC, 5MC, 5M, 19, 101, 111, 114, 116,
118, 121, 124, 126, 130
Cover Picture: Shutterstock

Distribution
UK, Ireland and Europe: Apa Publications (UK)
Ltd; sales@insightguides.com
United States and Canada: Ingram Publisher
Services; ips@ingramcontent.com
Australia and New Zealand: Woodslane;
info@woodslane.com.au
Southeast Asia: Apa Publications (SN) Pte;
singaporeoffice@insightguides.com
Hong Kong, Taiwan and China: Apa Publications
(HK) Ltd; hongkongoffice@insightguides.com
Worldwide: Apa Publications (UK) Ltd;
sales@insightguides.com

**Special Sales, Content Licensing
and CoPublishing**
Insight Guides can be purchased in bulk
quantities at discounted prices. We can create
special editions, personalised jackets and
corporate imprints tailored to your needs.
sales@insightguides.com;
www.insightguides.biz

Contact us
Every effort has been made to provide accurate
information in this publication, but changes are
inevitable. The publisher cannot be responsible
for any resulting loss, inconvenience or injury.
We would appreciate it if readers would call our
attention to any errors or outdated information.
We also welcome your suggestions; please
contact us at: berlitz@apaguide.co.uk
www.insightguides.com/berlitz